PASSOVER HAGGADAH

הגדה של פסח

A Messianic Celebration
arranged by
Eric-Peter Lipson

Published by
Purple Pomegranate Productions
San Francisco, California

Jews for Jesus, San Francisco 94102

Published 1986. Second Edition 1988
Printed in the United States of America
01 00 99 98   5 4 3 2

Illustrations and Cover Design
  by Naomi Dauermann

Library of Congress Cataloging in Publication Data

Lipson, Eric-Peter
  Passover Haggadah.

  Bibliography: p.
  1. Passover - Christian observance. I. Haggadah
II. Title
BV199.P25L57   1986   265'.9   85-82168
ISBN 0-9616148-1-1   Hardcover
ISBN 0-9616145-8-4   Paperback

Dedication

Zecher Tsaddikim Liv'rachah

The Remembrance of Righteous Ones Continues to Bless

To the Memory of my Parents
Major the Reverend Solomon Lipson, H.C.F.
and
Tilly Lipson

and to the honored memory of Mrs. James
Finn and her family, who in love for my
people planted the seed; and to that of
the Reverend Professor Jakob Jocz who,
having reaped where they sowed,
encouraged me to lead Messianic Jewish
Sedarim; with thanksgiving also for the
many Jews and Gentiles who by life and
by example have in love drawn me near
to Y'shua ha-Mashiach, especially in
gratitude to Irene, my dear wife.

TRANSLITERATION OF THE HEBREW

a   as in father

ai   as in aisle, to rhyme with file

ay   as in bay

e   as in bend

ee   as in creed

i   as in big

o   as in pole or poll

oo   as in boot

u   as in put

'   as e in her (a short-sounded emission of breath)

The transliteration is intended to be close to the Hebrew commonly spoken in Israel.

Accented syllables are in bold italic typeface.

The "ch" sound is always pronounced as in the Scottish word "loch," never as in "child."

PART I

PART I

A MESSIANIC CELEBRATION ברך א

1

This *haggadah* follows the pattern of the *seder,* the Passover Eve service held in Jewish homes, so that we may better understand how Jesus—Y'shua—boy and man—observed the festival, particularly at the Last Supper. Many prayers and blessings in this liturgy were known to him. As we say or chant them in Hebrew or in Aramaic (his mother tongue) we may hear sounds similar to those that were on his lips, and praise the Father in phrases our Lord used. We also see that many of his sayings are related to and in the form of rabbinic comments and interpretations of the Passover meal and its ritual.

The symbols on the table help us realize what Passover has always meant to the Jewish people. Enriched by Christian insights, the Festival of Freedom becomes a universal thanksgiving for redemption.

Participating in Passover ceremonies with his fellow Jews, Jesus celebrated Israel's deliverance from Egypt. Centuries after that event, he took common food — unleavened bread and festival wine — and distributing them as spiritual food, he vested these Passover symbols with enhanced significance giving additional cause for gratitude and thanksgiving. Passover, the season of Israel's liberation from bodily slavery, was transformed into a season of spiritual regeneration and redemption, whereby man could be freed from the slavery of sin. Peter and Paul sum up Jewish idealism and Christian purpose: "a chosen generation, a royal priesthood, a holy nation"; "we should no longer be slaves of sin" (I Peter 2:9 and Romans 6:6. See also Exodus 19:5-6).

Therefore, this haggadah is a synthesis of Christian and Jewish insights. Both Old and New Testaments—the whole Scripture—are here allied in the traditional form of a Passover seder. This haggadah may then be used as a basis for pre-Easter services and for messianic Passover celebrations. We hope also that it may serve to bring us near to Jesus, both at Communion and whenever we break bread each day at home.

3

There is much more material here than can be used at any one seder. Apart from basic essentials indicated in the text, celebrants are free to adapt (a) the time available before the main meal is served, (b) the length of the meal, preferably no longer than 45-50 minutes, and (c) time remaining for Communion, other prayers and some concluding songs. They may wish to add comments arising from personal insights, experience or family traditions in addition to or in place of those included in this haggadah. They would do well to preserve the traditional tunes and chants known and loved since childhood. From any one *piyyut* (liturgical poem) many chants have sprung into life. These help to preserve and renew family life and unity.

The *Mishnah* tells us that "no man is free but one who occupies himself in the study of *Torah*." Within the framework of the seder we are free to explore heavenly truths in the light of all Scripture.

THE MEANING OF PASSOVER

Pesach (plural Pesachim)

The word "pesach" may refer to any of the following:

1. The whole festival of Passover.
2. Specifically to the paschal lamb.
3. The special peace offerings of the festival.
4. A Passover meal.

In Israel the festival is observed for seven days, elsewhere by Orthodox Jews for eight, starting from the evening of 14th/15th Nisan, formerly known as *Abib*, the first month of the Jewish year (Exodus 12:2, 34:18). During the festival nothing leavened may be eaten or retained in Jewish homes; the only bread partaken is unleavened— *matzah* (plural *matzot*). Before the festival all leaven has been searched out and discarded (Exodus 13:7).

Before Israel's departure from Egypt, the first paschal lambs were slain, roasted and eaten by the Israelites in the following manner: "with a belt on your waist, your sandals on your feet, and your staff in your hand. So you shall eat it in haste. It is the LORD'S Passover" (Exodus 12:11). With sprigs of hyssop the blood was sprinkled on lintels and doorposts as a sign of faith in the Lord, who would pass over Israelite houses and not allow the Destroyer to enter and slay (Exodus 12:23).

In later years (with lapses) until 70 A.D., when the Temple at Jerusalem was destroyed by the Romans, the pesach, having been selected on the 10th Nisan, was slain on the 14th Nisan, its blood sprinkled against the altar in the Tabernacle or Temple at the place chosen by the Lord (Deuteronomy 16:6). The lamb, or kid, was a firstling male without blemish. Every person who was to partake of it was designated, so that each one acknowledged faith in God and in God's works of deliverance. At least 10 persons and as many as 99 could partake of this one lamb, religious duty being fulfilled if each ate a piece at least the size of an olive. The paschal lamb, partaken with matzah and bitter herb, was the last item eaten at the Passover meal. Any of it left over was to be burned.

To satisfy the hunger of those who reclined at the meal as freed folk enjoying ease from slavery, a freewill offering—the *chagigah* of 14th Nisan—was provided. Like the paschal lamb, it was roasted, unblemished firstling lamb or kid that could be added to the menu and was disposed of before the pesach was eaten. The roasted egg on the traditional Passover dish symbolizes both this chagigah festival offering and another chagigah that was eaten on the 15th Nisan.

Synoptic Gospels and John's Gospel Reconciled

The obligatory Passover peace offering, the second chagigah of 15th Nisan—also referred to as "pesach"— must be distinguished from the paschal lamb itself and its accompanying chagigah of the 14th Nisan (Deuteronomy 16:2-7, 16-17). In the Talmud a question is asked: "What is the meaning of Pesachim?" The reply is: "The Peace Offerings (*sh'lamim*) of Pesach" (Rosh Hashanah 5a).

It seems reasonable, therefore, that John 18:28, referring to "passover," means not the paschal lamb but the paschal peace offerings prepared and eaten during the *day* of 15th Nisan. These offerings could be taken from flock or herd, be male or female and, unlike the paschal lamb, could be boiled. Compare II Chronicles 35:13: "they roasted the Passover offerings with fire according to the ordinance; but the other holy offerings they boiled in pots."

In accordance with Genesis 1:5, a day begins at eventide. Jesus and the disciples came to recline at the Last Supper as freed men when 15th Nisan began. On that same day he was bound and beaten like a slave, and then crucified. For the priests it was a busy day; they were anxious to get on with the preparation and eating of the peace offerings and other sacrifices, and needed to avoid defilement at the governor's residence when they went to Pilate soon after dawn. Their relief that the Romans were to execute Jesus was marred by Pilate's contemptuous, "Behold your King," and by the royal title he had inscribed on the cross (John 19:14, 19). It was, moreover, the eve of the sabbath, with much else to do in preparation before darkness fell. Unexpectedly, there was darkness over all the land while Jesus hung on the cross during the last three hours of his agony. Thus, he completed his work for humanity's *re*creation on that sixth day of the week before God's hallowed day of rest.

On the first day of the week Y'shua rose from the tomb where he had rested to work again in a new way within the hearts of his followers, to show that redemption was a spiritual as well as a physical state for those made free.

The phrases "that they might eat the Passover" (John 18:28) and "the Preparation Day of the Passover" (John 19:14), have persuaded some scholars to conclude that this Gospel is at variance with the Synoptics. This is not so if the above interpretations are correct. The priests and Temple officials would have eaten the paschal lambs while Y'shua was with the disciples in the upper room.

Those who sought to arrest Jesus were free to go to Gethsemane on completion of their seder before midnight, after which the paschal lambs could not be eaten.

Even if it were shown that the priests and Y'shua ate the paschal lamb on different nights, the two narratives could be reconciled on the basis that Y'shua knew, by personal observation or through reliable witnesses, that the new moon had been seen at a time earlier than noted by Temple-certified witnesses. Latitude could make a great difference. Jewry was often divided as to the day when the new moon was first seen. If reliable witnesses saw the new moon even a minute or so one side or the other of nightfall, the first of the month could be proclaimed by a whole day's difference, thus affecting the dates of festivals.

A famous example is the dispute between Rabban Gamaliel II, president of the Sanhedrin, and the vice-president, Rabbi Joshua, at the end of the first century A.D. The former, asserting his view and authority, ordered the latter to travel to him on the day that Joshua had declared to be the sacred Day of Atonement, Sabbath of Sabbaths. Rabbi Joshua submitted, but their incensed colleagues deposed Gamaliel. Rabbi Elazar ben Azaryah,[1] a great scholar who, it is said, looked too young for the post, was elected in his place. According to legend, overnight he grew a suitably long, white beard! "I was like one seventy years old," he declared, "yet did not understand why the story of the Exodus had to be told at night, until Ben Zoma explained the verse, 'That you may remember the day you came out of Egypt all the days of your life.' *All* indicates night as well as day." Other sages interpreted it thus: "The days of your life" refers to this world; "all the days of your life" includes the days of the Messiah. This example of rabbinic exegesis included in the traditional haggadah is a reminder that Jewry has long expected the Messiah to appear at Passover.

Seder—Order of The Passover Meal

Arranged in a particular order—in Hebrew "seder"—the Passover eve meal has varied little in essentials for many centuries.[2] To preserve the knowledge of traditional practices, a written outline was completed circa 220 A.D. in the first part of the Talmud known as the Mishnah. Here are recorded the memories of Passover as observed before 70 A.D. when the Temple was destroyed and sacrifices could no longer be offered. Ceremonies and regulations were carefully noted so that again, when the time came, "the offering of Judah and Jerusalem will be pleasant to the Lord, as in the days of old, as in former years." This quotation from Malachi 3:4 is still prayed by Orthodox Jews three times daily. The seder as described in the Mishnah is in essence much like one practiced today, although later generations have added prayers, poems and exegetical material.

The seder liturgy narrates the events of the first Passover in Egypt and describes the symbols of the festival in such a way that both children and adults can witness to the power and glory of God in all he has done and is doing to redeem his people. The whole family is involved in the seder. Consequently, although it is a solemn affirmation of corporate faith—a link with our ancestors who have tasted God's goodness as well as a link with future generations—it is also a festival of fun and joy. Every household cherishes its own family stories and traditions that bind those who celebrate today with those who long ago rejoiced at this "season of our freedom," and with those yet unborn who will observe the Passover. The seder reminds us of our role as the people to whom have been entrusted the oracles of God. It also serves to remind us that God has not rejected his people whom he foreknew; "the gifts and the calling of God are irrevocable" (Romans 11:29). It is a special cause for thanksgiving when those already near, as partakers of God's promises, are joined in praise of the Almighty by those Gentiles who once were far off (Ephesians 2:13-14).

It is good to be part of the extended people of God through Y'shua ha-Mashiach. The Messiah "has become a servant to the circumcision for the truth of God, to confirm the promises made to the fathers, and that the Gentiles might glorify God for His mercy," rejoicing "with His people" (Romans 15:8-10).

PASSOVER SYMBOLS ON THE SEDER TABLE

Reminders of the ancient sacrifices—a bone of lamb and an egg, both roasted—are displayed side by side on the Passover dish (*k'arah*) with other festival symbols.

The lamb bone (*z'roah*, meaning arm) recalls the paschal lamb which no longer may be sacrificed. To emphasize the fact, it is customary not to eat lamb at the seder, lest we come to think we are actually partaking of the Passover sacrifice. If possible we use a shank bone in recollection of God's outstretched arm to save his people (Deuteronomy 26:8).

The egg (*betzah*) is usually referred to as "chagigah" (festival offering). It recalls two sacrifices: one killed on 14th Nisan and eaten at the seder before the paschal lamb (Pesachim 70a); the other slain during the *day* of 15th Nisan, or possibly later that week, as a freewill offering, each family bringing what it could afford to rejoice before the Lord and to match God's bounty. Similar peace offerings were brought by pilgrims at Pentecost and Tabernacles (Deuteronomy 16:16-17). These were taken from flock or herd and eaten roasted or boiled.[3]

Why should an egg represent such a sacrifice? It is a sign of mourning and a symbol of the hope of spiritual restoration and of resurrection. Jewry mourns the destruction of the Temple. Christians mourn that our sins brought Jesus to death on the cross.

The bitter herb (*maror*) symbolizes the bitterness of slavery, and in response we are grateful to God the Deliverer. God's people should harbor no root of bitterness. Memories of sufferings, ill-usage and disappointments must be healed. Yet we look to the day when "they will look on Me [Y'shua] whom they have pierced; they will mourn for Him as one mourns for his only son, and grieve for Him as one grieves for a firstborn . . . In that day a fountain shall be opened for the house of David and for the inhabitants of Jerusalem, for sin and for uncleanness" (Zechariah 12:10; 13:1).

Usually two kinds of maror are placed on the k'arah. Young shoots of horseradish or small slivers cut from the root are suitable for dipping into *charoset*. For the sandwich of matzah (*korech*) and bitter herb, many use grated horseradish. Others use lettuce, wrapping it around the matzah as tradition has it Hillel used to do. He, of course, included lamb in the sandwich.

Exodus 12:8 refers to m'rorim (herbs in the plural). It seems fitting that the second dish of maror should be home-grated, tear producing! Preferably prepared by the master of the household, it may help him empathize with how hard his wife worked to make the seder a culinary success and truly *pesachdik*. Surely she sheds enough tears during the year for all her household anxieties. Let this night be different from all other nights!

Salt water symbolizes the blood of the first paschal lambs sprinkled on Israelite lintels and doorposts before the Exodus, as well as tears shed by Israelite slaves and Jesus' tears when he wept over Jerusalem (Luke 19:41). We also recall Israel's baptism in the Sea of Reeds (Red Sea) as noted in Exodus 14:22.

Parsley (*karpas*) reminds us that hyssop, a cleansing herb, was dipped in the blood for the sprinkling. Had any Israelites failed to give this public expression of faith in God, they would have suffered the consequences when the Angel of Death passed through Egypt. However, Scripture indicates that every Israelite obeyed God's command (Exodus 12:28). No defaulter is mentioned. So Israel, cleansed from the sin of faithlessness, was ready for God's saving act of redemption. "Purge me with hyssop, and I shall be clean" (Psalm 51:7). We recall that hyssop accompanied the sponge of wine put to Jesus' lips just before he died bearing the sins of the world (John 19:29), and that his blood cleanses us from all sin (I John 1:7).

Charoset is a mixture of fruit-spice-wine-nuts eaten with the bitter herb to make it palatable. Basically charoset symbolizes clay, or the mud from which Israel made bricks to build store-cities for Pharoah. Including cinnamon sticks reminds us of the straw and stubble that the slaves had to gather to help bind the clay. The spices bring to mind those that were brought for Jesus' burial.

Unleavened Bread — Matzah

Bedikat Chametz — Search for Leaven

No leavened bread is eaten at Passover: "in all your habitations you shall eat unleavened bread" (Exodus 12:18-20). All leaven is removed from the home: "nor shall leaven be seen among you in all your quarters" (Exodus 13:7). By leaven—*chametz*—is meant the fermentation of barley, wheat, rye, oats or spelt, rather than of grapes or other fruit.

The evening before the seder, the beginning of 14th Nisan, "the first day of Unleavened Bread, when they killed the Passover lamb" (Mark 14:12, see also Exodus 12:6, 15, 18), the master of the house searches by candlelight for any crumbs remaining after his wife has scrupulously cleaned the whole house. A kindly spouse, as my mother was, will place a morsel or two of leaven at a strategic point in each room, such as a corner of the mantelpiece. Then her husband may sweep it away with a feather into a wooden spoon and have maximum satisfaction in carrying out God's ordinance by actually finding apparently overlooked chametz. If mother occasionally places the offending crumbs in an unusual spot, it is amusing for the children to see dad hunting for chametz without immediate success, and to hear his "Nu! Nu!" of inquiry or exasperation; for during the performance of the *mitzvah*—the God-given commandment—he is not permitted to speak, only to concentrate on the act.

Early the next morning, all leaven found is burned. Both Gentile and Jewish children in Whitechapel, London, used to carry pierced tin buckets containing burning coals. As they passed along the streets, loudly crying, "Chametz," the householders responded by bringing out their leaven to be burned, paying a few coppers for the service. (The Jewish boys spent this wealth on cobnuts to play a game like marbles.)

Utensils used daily are most rigorously cleaned or, alternatively, set aside during Passover week. Many observant Jews keep sets of utensils, crockery and cutlery reserved for Passover use only.

Three Matzot

A cloth bag divided into three compartments holds three special matzot: one in the center compartment, the other two above and below. The outermost matzot recall the double portion of manna (*lechem mishneh*) gathered every sixth day, Sabbath eve, by Israel in the wilderness (Exodus 16:14-31). The central matzah recalls the Bread of Affliction (*lechem onee*), Humble Bread, or the Poor Bread. Because when the Temple stood, the paschal lamb was eaten only within the walls of Jerusalem, something of the lamb's mystique was attached to the lechem onee everywhere outside the Holy City. It was considered a token of the Coming One—the Messiah—who would deliver the people from foreign oppression.[4]

Jesus, in John 6, seems to identify himself with lechem onee, but he sees beyond mere physical national deliverance: " 'I am the bread of life . . . come down from heaven. . . . Your fathers ate the manna in the wilderness, and are dead. This is the bread which comes down from heaven, that one may eat of it and not die. I am the living bread which came down from heaven . . . the bread that I shall give is My flesh, which I shall give for the life of the world'" (John 6:35, 38, 49-51). He said this while teaching in the synagogue as he taught in Capernaum (v. 59). Verses 53-58 in particular should be deeply significant to us as we eat lechem onee.[5]

Salt of the Covenant

The presence of a dish of salt teaches us that all who sit at the table should feel that table to be as sacred as an altar dedicated to God: "This is the table that is before the LORD" (Ezekiel 41:22). According to Rabbi Simeon ben Yochai,[6] this verse underlines the thought that when we discuss God's Word at mealtime, it is as if we eat at the table of the All-Present (Aboth 3:4). Every day each meal becomes a thank-offering.

"You shall not allow the salt of the covenant of your God to be lacking from your grain offering. With all your offerings you shall offer salt" (Leviticus 2:13). So bread is dipped in salt three times as the grace before a meal is said—three times in order that we concentrate on the thought that God is faithful to his covenants, as we should be. Salt is a symbol of preservation, purity and steadfast fellowship. "'Have salt in yourselves'" (Mark 9:50). "'You are the salt of the earth'" (Matthew 5:13)—if you do God's will by displaying integrity, faithfulness and grace to the world, but above all, love.

Wine

Four Cups of Promise . . . and a Fifth

God heard . . . God remembered . . . God saw . . . God cared (Exodus 2:24-25), so he made promises and said to Moses:

Therefore . . . say to the children of Israel:
"I am the LORD;
I will bring you out from under the burdens of the Egyptians,
I will rescue you from their bondage, and
I will redeem you with an outstretched arm and with great judgments.
I will take you as My people, and I will be your God. Then you shall know that I am the LORD your God who brings you out from under the burdens of the Egyptians. And I will bring you into the land which I swore to give to Abraham, Isaac, and Jacob; and I will give it to you as a heritage: I am the LORD" (Exodus 6:6-8).

In remembrance of these four promises, we drink four cups of wine, for in the ancient world freed slaves would be given "wine-bowls of freedom."

1. I will bring you out.
The Cup of Sanctification (*Kiddush*) at the beginning of the seder.

2. I will rescue you.
The Cup of Telling-forth, of Praise and of Deliverance, taken after the singing of the first part (Psalm 113-114) of the Hallel before the main meal. Luke 22:17-18 refers to this cup or, possibly, to the Kiddush cup.

15

3. I will redeem you.

The Cup of Blessing and Redemption, taken after the meal (Matthew 26:27; Mark 14:23; Luke 22:20; I Corinthians 10:16).

4. I will take you as My people.

The Cup of Completion taken towards the end of the seder: I will take you as My people and be your God and you shall know that I am God.

". . . no one can say that Jesus is Lord except by the Holy Spirit" (I Corinthians 12:3). We remember that on the cross Jesus said, " 'I thirst,' " received wine and, his atoning work completed, cried, " 'It is finished'" (John 19:28, 30).

The Cup of Elijah. A fifth cup used to be taken, relating, perhaps to the promises concerning the Promised Land. When Israel was exiled from the land, the cup was filled, but not drunk. It remained on the table as a sign of God's further messianic promise of renewal, " 'I will send you Elijah the prophet'" (Malachi 4:5) and of other promises of restoration (e.g. Deuteronomy 30:1-6). Legend declares that Elijah visits every Jewish home at the seder and sips the cup. We recall Jesus saying, " 'Elijah has also come'" (Mark 9:13). This was certainly true in the person of John the Baptist (Matthew 11:14).

PREPARATION FOR THE LAST SUPPER

A synthesis of
Matthew 26:17-20; Mark 14:12-17; Luke 22:7-13

On the first day of Unleavened Bread, when they sacrificed the Passover lamb, his disciples came to Jesus saying, "'Where will you have us go and prepare for you to eat the pesach, the paschal lamb?'" He sent two of his disciples,

Peter and John, saying to them, "'Go and prepare the paschal lamb for us that we may eat it.'" They said, "'Where will you have us get ready?'" He said to them, "Go into the city (Jerusalem). When you have entered, a man carrying a pitcher of water will meet you; follow him into whatever house he enters and say to the householder, 'The Rabbi says, "My time is at hand. I will keep the Passover at your house; where is the guestroom where I am to eat the paschal lamb with my disciples?"' He will show you a large upper room, furnished and prepared. There make ready for us." The disciples did as Jesus directed them, set out and went into the city and found all as he had told them.

Then they prepared the paschal lamb.

On the 10th Nisan, the day that Jesus rode into Jerusalem on an ass, Peter and John selected a yearling lamb without blemish and killed it in the Temple on the first day of Unleavened Bread. They made it ready for roasting, skewered with pomegranate wood thrust through from mouth to buttocks (Mishnah *Pesachim* 7:1). They would also have prepared the usual festival sacrifice (chagigah) in accordance with Deuteronomy 16:16-17.

Presumably they roasted the lamb either in the roof-chamber of the house or in one of the many ovens in the city's open places made available for the use of pilgrims.

At nightfall the festival day began. Jesus sat down, and the twelve disciples with him. There was no immediate danger of arrest, for all Temple officials would have been intent on observing the Passover meal ceremonies themselves.

When towards the end of the meal the paschal lamb was set before Jesus, he said to them, "With fervent desire I have desired to eat this [paschal lamb] with you before I suffer; for I say to you, I will no longer eat of it until it is fulfilled in the kingdom of God" (Luke 22:15-16). This may mean either "Despite my great desire, I shall not eat the paschal lamb with you," or "This is the last time I shall eat it with you."

Did Jesus partake of the paschal lamb? Scripture does not give a clear answer. No doubt he partook of the other festival fare, but at the end of the meal did he eat the paschal lamb when he broke the bread and gave it to his disciples? Similarly, the two statements: (1) before the main meal, "'Take this [cup] and divide it among yourselves; for I say to you, I will not drink of the fruit of the vine until the kingdom of God comes'" (Luke 22:17-18) and (2) after supper, "'I will no longer drink of the fruit of the vine . . .'" (Mark 14:25; see also Matthew 26:29) suggest that perhaps Jesus did not drink of the Cup of Thanksgiving, nor of the Cup of Blessing. We cannot be sure.

PART II

PART II

A MESSIANIC CELEBRATION

ברך

Festival Lights

According to tradition, the Israelites were redeemed from Egypt because of the pious women of that generation, considered to be more righteous than the men. It is therefore a woman's privilege to kindle sabbath and festival lights in the home (Sotah 11b).

(The Mother of the Company lights the candles, gives thanks and asks for blessing on those present and all dear to her:)

Blessed art Thou, O Lord our God, King of the Universe, who has sent Thy Son, Thine Only Son, Y'shua the Messiah, to be the light of the world and our Paschal Lamb, that through him we might live. Amen.

בָּרוּךְ אַתָּה יְיָ אֱלֹהֵינוּ מֶלֶךְ הָעוֹלָם שֶׁשָּׁלַח
אֶת בִּנְךָ יְחִידְךָ יֵשׁוּעַ הַמָּשִׁיחַ לִהְיוֹת אוֹר
הָעוֹלָם וְשֶׂה הַפֶּסַח שֶׁלָּנוּ לְמַעַן נִחְיֶה בִּזְכוּתוֹ.
אָמֵן:

Baruch ata Adonai Elohaynu melech ha-olam, sheshalach et bin'cha y'chid'cha, Y'shua Ha-Mashiach, lih'yot or ha-olam v'seh happesach shelanu l'ma-an nich'yeh biz'chuto. Amen.

(Silent Prayer.)

Children's Blessing

(Father, or Celebrant, blessing the children,
says to the sons:)

The Lord make thee like Ephraim and Manasseh
and like Peter, Andrew, John and the other disciples who
truly followed Jesus.

(Then to the daughters:)

The Lord make thee like Sarah, Rebekah, Rachel
and Leah and like Susannah, Joanna and the other faithful
women who ministered to Jesus.

(To each he gives also the Aaronic blessing:)

The Lord bless thee and keep thee,
The Lord cause His Presence to shine upon thee
and be gracious unto thee,
The Lord turn His face towards thee and give thee
wholeness, peace, *shalom.*

יְבָרֶכְךָ יְיָ וְיִשְׁמְרֶךָ: יָאֵר יְיָ פָּנָיו אֵלֶיךָ וִיחֻנֶּךָ:
יִשָּׂא יְיָ פָּנָיו אֵלֶיךָ וְיָשֵׂם לְךָ שָׁלוֹם:

Y'varech'cha Adonai v'yishm'recha
Ya-ayr Adonai panav aylecha veechunnekka
Yissa Adonai panav aylecha v'yasaym l'cha
shalom (Numbers 6:24-26).

Kiddush — Sanctification

(Raise the first cup.)

"I Will Bring You Out"

Throughout his life, Jesus would have begun every sabbath and festival day with an act of sanctification,
remembering his Father as Creator, Giver of Rest, and
Redeemer, praising God for wine that makes glad the
heart of man and for bread that strengthens man's heart
(Psalm 104:15).

At the beginning of this evening we rededicate ourselves to God so that during the seder, hearts and minds seek to realize fully all we owe God for his goodness and redeeming power and for the many ways God has blessed his people.

Blessed be the Lord our God, King of the Universe, who has given us gifts of grace, not through our merits, but only because of his abounding love and mercy, and has called us to proclaim good news of salvation for all who turn to him.

We thank him for giving us this Passover festival to remind us of our deliverance from Egyptian bondage, and for showing love to all people by sending Jesus into the world to save mankind from the slavery of sin (John 8:34).

Blessed be the Lord who cleanses and sanctifies us through the life, teaching and sacrifice of our Lord Jesus the Messiah. Amen.

Blessed art Thou, O Lord our God, King of the Universe, who createst the fruit of the vine.

בָּרוּךְ אַתָּה יְיָ אֱלֹהֵינוּ מֶלֶךְ הָעוֹלָם בּוֹרֵא פְּרִי הַגָּפֶן:

Baruch ata Adonai Elohaynu melech ha-olam boray p'ree haggafen.

(Drink the first cup.)

A General Thanksgiving

This blessing is said often in the course of the year to mark the initiation of something; for example, the beginning of a festival, on eating any fruit for the first time in its season, entering into possession of a new home, on wearing new clothes for the first time. It is no surprise to find that when we thank God for benefits, fruit has better flavor, clothing gives more pleasure, and celebrations hold greater enjoyment—"giving thanks always for all things to God" (Ephesians 5:20).

25

Blessed art Thou, O Lord our God, King of the Universe, who hast kept us alive and sustained us, and brought us to this season.

בָּרוּךְ אַתָּה יְיָ אֱלֹהֵינוּ מֶלֶךְ הָעוֹלָם שֶׁהֶחֱיָנוּ
וְקִיְּמָנוּ וְהִגִּיעָנוּ לַזְּמַן הַזֶּה:

Baruch ata Adonai Elohaynu melech ha-olam she-heche-yanu v'kee-y'manu v'higgee-anu laz'man hazzeh.

(The Company may wish to sing:)

Rejoice in the Lord always
And again I say, rejoice   (Repeat)

Rejoice, rejoice,
And again I say, rejoice   (Repeat)[A]

Ur'Chatz

(Celebrant may wash.)[7]

Karpas — Parsley for Hyssop

(Dip the parsley into the salt water and say:)

"And you shall take a bunch of hyssop, dip it in the blood that is in the basin, and strike the lintel and the two doorposts with the blood that is in the basin" (Exodus 12:22a).

Blessed art Thou, O Lord our God, King of the Universe, who createst the fruit of the ground.

בָּרוּךְ אַתָּה יְיָ אֱלֹהֵינוּ מֶלֶךְ הָעוֹלָם בּוֹרֵא פְּרִי
הָאֲדָמָה:

Baruch ata Adonai Elohaynu melech ha-olam boray p'ree ha'adama.

The sprinkling of the blood ratifying God's covenant with Israel (Exodus 24:8) served both as expiation for past faithlessness and as a sign of renewal of trust. The Messiah is both the true paschal lamb (I Corinthians 5:7)

26

and the sin sacrifice burned outside Israel's camp (Hebrews 13:11-13). Jesus, the Lamb of God, the Suffering Servant, suffered outside the city gate to expiate sin and to sanctify the people by his blood. He was also our Peace Offering, for while he was on the cross, the other pesachim — the peace offerings of the festival (sh'lamim)—were being sacrificed (John 18:28). Y'shua is our peace; Jew and Gentile are united in him (Ephesians 2:12-14).

Yachatz

(Break in two the middle cake of matzah, the Bread of Affliction. The larger piece, the *aphikoman*, is to be wrapped in a cloth and hidden and will be eaten at the end of the meal as we remember Jesus saying to his disciples, "Take, eat." The smaller portion which is eaten at the beginning of the meal is now held up by the Celebrant who recites in Aramaic, Jesus' mother tongue, the traditional invitation:

Declaration and Invitation

הָא לַחְמָא עַנְיָא דִי אֲכָלוּ אֲבָהָתָנָא בְּאַרְעָא
דְמִצְרָיִם. כָּל דִכְפִין יֵיתֵי וְיֵיכוּל, כָּל דִצְרִיךְ
יֵיתֵי וְיִפְסַח, הָשַׁתָּא הָכָא, לְשָׁנָה הַבָּאָה
בְּאַרְעָא דְיִשְׂרָאֵל הָשַׁתָּא עַבְדֵי, לְשָׁנָה הַבָּאָה
בְּנֵי חוֹרִין:

Ha lachma anya dee achalu avahatana b'ar-a d'mitzra-yim. Kol dichfin yay-tay v'yaychul, kol dit-zreech yay-tay v'yifsach. Hashatta hacha, l'shanah habba-ah b'ar-a d'yisrael. Hashatta avday l'shanah habba-ah b'nay chorin.

This is the Bread of Affliction which our forefathers ate in the land of Egypt. Let all who are hungry come and eat. Let all who are in need come and celebrate the Passover. Many today are enslaved by sin and many by oppressors. May all be made free through Y'shua ha-Mashiach.[8]

(Replace the bread; fill the second cup.)

I Will Rescue You From Bondage

"This is the Bread of Affliction," or "this is like the Bread of Affliction": Most haggodot follow the first phrase; some, for rational reasons, the latter. How could it be the very bread our forefathers baked and ate so many centuries ago? Yet those who prefer the former phrase, commonly used before Jesus was born, do not believe that anything wonderful or mystic has happened to the matzah. Rather, they hold that as we look at the matzah and identify with our afflicted ancestors, we seek to understand their hopelessness and plight as slaves. Then, when we eat the aphikoman at the end of the meal, we better appreciate all that God has done for us as Deliverer and Savior, and with greater thankfulness enjoy the freedom God has given us.

Mah Nishtanah—Four Questions

We can well believe that the women who came with Jesus from Galilee were present at the Last Supper. One likes to think that one of their children asked the customary four questions, much like those to be asked this evening.

(The youngest person present asks:)

מַה נִּשְׁתַּנָּה הַלַּיְלָה הַזֶּה מִכָּל הַלֵּילוֹת: שֶׁבְּכָל
הַלֵּילוֹת אָנוּ אוֹכְלִין חָמֵץ וּמַצָּה הַלַּיְלָה הַזֶּה כֻּלּוֹ
מַצָּה. שֶׁבְּכָל הַלֵּילוֹת אָנוּ אוֹכְלִין שְׁאָר יְרָקוֹת
הַלַּיְלָה הַזֶּה מָרוֹר. שֶׁבְּכָל הַלֵּילוֹת אֵין אָנוּ
מַטְבִּילִין אֲפִילוּ פַּעַם אֶחָת, הַלַּיְלָה הַזֶּה שְׁתֵּי
פְּעָמִים. שֶׁבְּכָל הַלֵּילוֹת אָנוּ אוֹכְלִין בֵּין יוֹשְׁבִין
וּבֵין מְסֻבִּין, הַלַּיְלָה הַזֶּה כֻּלָּנוּ מְסֻבִּין:

Mah nishtanah hallailah hazzeh mikkol hallaylot? Shebb'chol hallaylot anu och'lin chametz

28

umatzah hallailah hazzeh kullo matzah. Shebb'chol hallaylot anu och'lin sh'ar y'rakot; hallailah hazzeh maror. Shebb'chol hallaylot ayn anu matbeelin afeelu pa-am echat; hallailah hazzeh sh'tay f'amim. Shebb'chol hallaylot anu och'lin bayn yosh'vin uvayn m'subin; hallailah hazzeh kulanu m'subin.

"Why is this night different from all other nights? Other nights we may eat either leavened or unleavened bread; this night only unleavened.

"Other nights we may eat any kind of herbs; tonight we must eat bitter herbs.

"Other nights we do not dip even once; tonight twice—parsley into salt water, and later on bitter herb into charoset.

"Other nights we eat sitting or reclining, as we please; tonight we should all recline."

Only those who are free reclined. Slaves sit to eat or stand, as did the Israelite slaves during their last meal in Egypt. Jesus at the Last Supper would have reclined upon cushions, leaning on his left elbow. John, too, lying close to his breast, could whisper, "'Lord, who is it?'", after Jesus had declared, "'One of you will betray me'" (John 13:23-25).

God Asks Us Four Questions

When at last we stand before the Almighty Judge, he will ask:
"Were you honest in business and labor?
"Did you fix a time to study Torah, my Words of Instruction?
"Did you build up family life?
"Have you trusted in Salvation through the Messiah?"

(Talmud, Shabbat 31a)

MAGGID — NARRATION
— FROM SHAME TO GLORY

(Celebrant, uncovering the matzot,
replies to the Mah Nishtanah:)

Avadim ha-yeenu l'pharob b'mitzra-yim . . .
Because in Egypt we were Pharoah's slaves,
But the Lord our God brought us out from that land
With outstretched arm and the strength of his hand;
And had the Holy One, blessed be he,
Not saved our ancestors from bondage then,
Neither we, nor our children, nor theirs, would be free;
Still being slaves—not as now, free—
We would serve in Egypt. Thank God who saves!

It is our duty to recount God's acts of deliverance,
to read and study his Holy Word; to remember that just as
God brought us from servitude in Egypt, so—through
Jesus—he frees us from the slavery of sin. The more we
meditate on these things, the more God gives us insights,
blessings and thankful hearts.

The story is told of five famous rabbis, so en-
grossed in discussing the Exodus that they failed to notice
when it was dawn and time, as their pupils reminded
them, to say the morning prayers.

The Four Sons

God's Word will call to mind four types of son:
The wise, the wicked, and the simple one,
The fourth who cannot ask why things are done.

The wise son questions the father thus:
"What mean these many laws to us
Our God has given?" Tell him all
There is to tell of the Festival

(Deuteronomy 6:20, LXX).

The bad son asks, "What's this to you,
The slavery of all you do?"
Then father answers sadly, "Lo!
It seems God's love you do not know;
He ransomed *me* long years ago."

The simple son cries, "Dad, what's this?"
Complexities you may dismiss,
But simply and with patience tell
How God delivered Israel.

And as for him who cannot ask,
The father has a happy task:
He takes the symbols one by one
And shows them to his silent son.

The wise son (*chacham*) associates himself with his family's worship of God: "What are these laws to *us*?" The wicked son (*rasha*) disassociates himself from the salvation that his father and the other members of the family acknowledge. He may be clever, but he despises godly zeal.

The simple (*tam*)—rather perhaps the innocent—son could be the best of the bunch. He requires an honest, straightforward, reasonable and satisfying explanation. Not as clever, maybe, as the other two, yet he is loyal and trustworthy—a good friend. He just wants to know what is right, so that he can serve God and his fellows as he should. "Tam" means "perfect, faultless." Of such a one, Jesus said, "Behold, an Israelite indeed, in whom is no guile!" (John 1:47)

The one who doesn't know how to ask (*she-ayno yodeya lish'ol*) may be shy, tongue-tied out of fear, or just too young. He must be put at ease, his interest roused. He should be encouraged, but not pressed, to take part and to open up. Tell him easy-to-remember stories and family jokes about Passover that he'll treasure all his life. He will come to love Pesach.

God's word, Torah, speaks *of* four sons who have to be taught the meaning of the Passover. It also speaks *to* them. God desires the wicked to repent, and to know and enjoy the Lord's salvation.

A Four-Son Pattern in Mark 12

In verses 13-17 of Mark 12, the Pharisees ask a question about taxes, as might a wise son. The mocking Sadducees, who do not believe in resurrection, afterlife or the Messiah, cynically inquire about life after death in verses 18-27. A simple scribe seeks to know how to conduct himself (v. 28-34), after which "no one dared question Him [Jesus]." Nevertheless, in the Temple he went on teaching those who dared not ask (v. 35-37).

We may think the wise son a type of Jesus to whom is revealed *all* the secret, mystic and heavenly implications of the aphikoman, which represents the expected Messiah. The explanation given to the wise son in the orthodox haggadah is utterly inadequate, i.e., that nothing is to be eaten after the paschal aphikoman. Even the youngest son would be told that. Only the wise son, able to understand the mystery of the Coming One, is instructed in secret lore. Yet he who is thought to be wise may lack godly wisdom: "Jesus rejoiced in the Spirit and said, 'I praise You, Father, Lord of heaven and earth, that You have hidden these things from the wise and prudent and revealed them to babes'" (Luke 10:21). To his disciples he said: "'it has been given to you to know the mysteries of the kingdom of heaven, but to them it has not been given . . . But blessed are your eyes for they see, and your ears for they hear'" (Matthew 13:11, 16). This reminds us of Deuteronomy 11:26-27: "Behold, I set before you today a blessing . . . if you obey the commandments of the LORD your God . . . ."

Formerly our ancestors served idols—Abraham's father Terah did (Joshua 24:2-4)—but God has brought us near to his service. Some of you, says Paul to the Corinthians, were formerly ungodly, "But you were washed, but you were sanctified, but you were justified in the name of the Lord Y'shua and by the Spirit of our God" (I Corinthians 6:11).

Blessed be He who always keeps His promise, as He did to Abraham.

(Raise the cup in remembrance
of God's faithfulness, and say:)

God's faithfulness when enemies conspired
To blot us out in ages past
Preserved our ancestors and always fired
Our hearts when evil cast
Its shadow. For the Holy One required
Our lives at tyrants' hands—and saved at last.

(Replace the cup.)

From Slavery To Redemption

Our fathers went down to Egypt with only 70 persons (Deuteronomy 10:22) and there we became a great nation (Deuteronomy 26:5).

But the Egyptians ill-treated us, afflicted us and laid heavy bondage upon us (Deuteronomy 26:6).

At length the king of Egypt, perhaps Ramses the Great, died, but the children of Israel still groaned under bondage. They cried out and their cry under bondage came up to God (Exodus 2:23).

"Then we cried out to the LORD God of our fathers, and the LORD heard our voice and looked on our affliction and our labor and our oppression" (Deuteronomy 26:7). "So God heard their groaning, and God remembered His covenant with Abraham, with Isaac, and with Jacob" (Exodus 2:24). God saw the children of Israel and knew their condition. He cared.

Moses the Levite, adopted son of an Egyptian princess, saw his people's burdens. In anger he slew a

taskmaster who was beating a slave. Later on he rebuked a Hebrew man who was smiting a fellow Hebrew. "'Who made you a prince and a judge over us? Do you intend to kill me as you killed the Egyptian?'" demanded the one who did the wrong. Moses fled to the land of Midian, for his deed was known and Pharaoh sought to slay him (Exodus 2:11-15). To the question, "Who made you a prince and a judge?" God gave his answer at the burning thornbush (Exodus 3).

Thus, thorns were associated with both this act of salvation and the Messiah's. When God appeared to Moses from the thornbush, it was as if the *Shechinah* (Holy Presence) wore a crown of thorns. The rabbis have seen this as a sign of God's sympathy: "My people are steeped in sorrow and their suffering has pierced my soul like a thorn" (Exodus Rabba, Shemot 2,5).[9]

When the suffering Messiah bore the crown of thorns, God again proclaimed his continuing personal concern and sympathy for his people.[10]

God's Love And Care Are Universal

God cares for all peoples, not only for Israel. "The LORD is gracious and full of compassion, slow to anger and great in mercy. The LORD is good to all, and His tender mercies are over all His works" (Psalm 145:8-9). "'Are you not like the people of Ethiopia to Me, O children of Israel?' says the LORD. 'Did I not bring up Israel from the land of Egypt, the Philistines from Caphtor, and the Syrians from Kir?'" (Amos 9:7) "You shall neither mistreat a stranger nor oppress him, for you were strangers in the land of Egypt . . . you know the heart of a stranger" (Exodus 22:21; 23:9).

God's Word teaches compassion toward one's enemies. So when each plague that afflicted the Egyptians is mentioned, a drop of wine from the newly poured Cup of Thanksgiving is spilled, preferably into a small "plague saucer." Thus when we drink the cup, the joy of our deliverance is tempered by sorrow that the Egyptians had to suffer because of the hardening of Pharaoh's heart.

These Are The Ten Plagues

. . . which the Holy One, Blessed be He, brought on the Egyptians in Egypt:

(As each is named, deposit a drop of wine into a saucer.)

1. Blood—*Dam*
2. Frogs—*Ts'farday-ah*
3. Gnats (lice)—*Kinnim*
4. Scarab Beetles (flies)— *'Arov*
5. Pestilence (diseased livestock)—*Dayvayr*
6. Boils—*Sh'chin*
7. Hail—*Barad*
8. Locusts—*Arbay*
9. Darkness—*Choshech*
10. Firstborn Slain—*Makkat B'chorot*

Yam Suph—The Sea of Reeds—The Red Sea

On the seventh day after the Exodus, Pharaoh's chariots and horses and all his host were trapped and drowned in the Sea of Reeds. According to a Jewish legend, angels then sang God's praises. He rebuked them: "The work of my hands, the creatures to whom I gave life, are drowned. When I weep that they are dead, do you sing praises to me who slew them?" (Sanhedrin 39b).

Isaiah reminds us of God's promise: "Then the Lord will be known to Egypt, and the Egyptians will know the Lord in that day . . . the Lord of hosts shall bless, saying, 'Blessed is Egypt My people, and Assyria the work of My hands, and Israel My inheritance'" (Isaiah 19:21-25). At least 60 times Ezekiel stresses God's determination that those who disobey his will, besides those who seek to serve him, "'shall know that I am the Lord.'"

Pharaoh himself survived. Today, says a *Midrash*, he stands at the gate of hell to ask each tyrant passing through, "Why did you not profit by my example?"

Some rabbis have argued that the Egyptians suffered more than 10 plagues. In Egypt the magicians said,

"This is the finger of God," whereas at the sea, Israel saw the great hand which the Lord laid against the Egyptians. Therefore one must assume that if there were 10 plagues in Egypt, at the sea there must have been 50! This speculation was capped by Rabbi Akiba who quoted Psalm 78:49, asserting that as God sent fierce anger, wrath, indignation, trouble and a band of evil angels, each plague consisted of five plagues. Thus he concluded that the Egyptians suffered 50 plagues in Egypt and 250 at the sea, for a grand total of 300!

The magnification of Egyptian disaster intends no more than to proclaim God's power to conquer all who oppose his will and refuse to reverence him. We are not to take pleasure in the humiliation of an oppressor. "Do not rejoice when your enemy falls, and do not let your heart be glad when he stumbles" (Proverbs 24:17).

Yet God has set a limit to his power, for he has given man free will. "Everything is in the power of Heaven except the fear, the reverence, of Heaven." (Berachot 33b). Yet God declares, "'I will put my fear in their hearts, that they will not depart from me'" (Jeremiah 32:40). There is no contradiction; God does not take away man's free will, nor does he force entry into an obdurate heart; but the moment one has a desire to serve the Lord, God graciously puts his fear into one's heart. God gives that person his treasure for "The fear of the Lord is His treasure" (Isaiah 33:6).

All glory and power belong to God. Exodus 14:31 witnesses, "Thus Israel saw the great work which the LORD had done in Egypt; so the people feared the LORD, and believed the LORD and His servant Moses." This is the only mention of Moses in the haggadah used in most Jewish homes. It emphasizes that deliverance from Egypt was divine, not human. Freedom from the slavery of sin, this also is God's doing. We cannot save ourselves. Praise Jesus!

So the traditional haggadah comments on Deuteronomy 26:8 and Exodus 12:12: "The Lord brought us from Egypt, not through angel, seraph or agent. He himself acted in his glory, as it is said, I will pass through

the land of Egypt that night (I, and not an Angel) and will smite every firstborn (I, and not a Seraph) and on all the gods of Egypt I will execute judgments (I, and not an Agent). I am the Lord (I am He and no other)."

Neither *mal'ach*, angel or messenger; nor seraph, wielder of heaven's mysterious forces; nor *shaliach*, agent sent by God, does the work of God. God uses them merely as tools in his hands, or as channels of his power, either of rebuke or grace. Even as he smites, it is in order that individuals and nations might know him and be reconciled to him.

The Almighty has done so much for us; any one of his gifts or saving acts would have been sufficient to evoke from our hearts thanks and praise.

(So we chant:)

Da-yenu

It would have been enough for us.

Celebrant	Company
Had he but brought us out of Egypt	*Da-yenu*
Had he judged the Egyptians	*Da-yenu*
And destroyed their gods	*Da-yenu*
Had he slain their firstborn	*Da-yenu*
And given us their riches	*Da-yenu*
Had he divided the sea to let us pass through	*Da-yenu*
But sank our foes into the depths	*Da-yenu*
Then supplied our needs for forty years	*Da-yenu*
And fed us with manna in the wilderness	*Da-yenu*
Had he given us the sabbath to renew our strength	*Da-yenu*
And brought us to hear him at Mount Sinai	*Da-yenu*
Giving us his Torah to guide us	*Da-yenu*
Planned and built the Tabernacle, his dwelling place	*Da-yenu*
Brought us to the land he promised to Israel	*Da-yenu*

41

Consecrated the Temple he permitted to be built	*Da-yenu*
Sent Jesus, the "Temple not built with hands"	*Da-yenu*
That atonement be made for all our sins.	*Da-Da-yenu* *(Sung)*

(And now in Hebrew we sing:)

Da-yenu

I - lu ho-tzi ho-tzi-o-nu, ho-tzi-o-nu mi-Mitz-ra-yim,

ho-tzi-o-nu mi-Mitz-ra-yim, da-ye-nu:

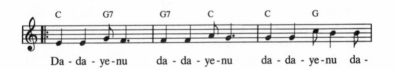

Da-da-ye-nu da-da-ye-nu da-da-ye-nu da-

ye-nu da-ye-nu da-ye-nu ye-nu da-ye-nu

In the traditional haggadah, as still recited by Orthodox Jewry, this ancient thanksgiving ends, "He built for us His chosen house to atone for all our sins." Yet Solomon's Temple, as God foretold, was to become a heap of ruins: "this house which I have sanctified for My name I will cast out of My sight" (I Kings 9·7).

"Jesus . . . said . . . 'Destroy this temple, and in three days I will raise it up.' . . . He was speaking of the temple of His body" (John 2:19, 21).

This poem, "Da-yenu," comments Dr. Cecil Roth, "reminds us that physical redemption from bondage is not complete unless accompanied by spiritual redemption. The building of the temple is thus the logical sequel of the Exodus."[B] We affirm, however, that the logical and actual sequel was the building of the Tabernacle at God's command, and then, when both Solomon's Temple and Herod's were no longer spiritually God's dwelling place, Jesus "tabernacled" in the midst of God's people; that through him atonement had been made for all our sins. Aaron, who ministered in the Tabernacle, God's earlier pattern, is said by the rabbis to have "loved peace and pursued peace, loved his fellow men and brought them nearer to the Torah" (Aboth 1:12). Jesus, the very Word of God, is the pattern shown to us. He, the Prince of Peace, is our peace.

Two Swords? Enough!

When the disciples showed Jesus two swords after the Passover meal, Jesus said, "It is enough" (*"Hikanon estin"* in Greek or "Da-yenu" in Hebrew) (Luke 22:38). He also rebuked Peter, who drew his sword in defense at Gethsemane, saying, "all who take the sword will perish by the sword" (Matthew 26:52; John 18:10-11). When Jesus said "Dayenu!" surely he spoke ironically; the disciples still did not understand. Perhaps he remembered Hillel's comment upon seeing a skull afloat in water: "Because you drowned others, they have drowned you. Those who drowned you will themselves be drowned" (Aboth 2:7).

Three Symbols Of The Feast

Hillel's grandson Gamaliel, president of the Sanhedrin and Paul's teacher warned his colleagues in the council against molesting the apostles whom they'd arrested: " 'Men of Israel, take heed to yourselves what you intend to do regarding these men . . . let them alone; for if this plan or this work is of men, it will come to nothing; but if it is of

God, you cannot overthrow it—lest you even be found to fight against God'" (Acts 5:34-35, 38-39).

The haggadah quotes Rabban Gamaliel as saying, "If we do not speak of and explain the meaning of these three Passover symbols, we fail in our duty: pesach, the paschal lamb; matzah, the unleavened bread; maror, the bitter herb" (Mishnah, Pesachim 10, 5).

The Unbroken Lamb-Bone and The Roasted Egg

This bone (z'roah) is a symbol of the paschal lamb slain in Egypt, its blood sprinkled on the doorposts as a sign that God's people trusted in him. It recalls the Lamb of God himself (John 1:29, 36), no bone of whom was broken, who died for our sins that we might have eternal life. The Messiah, our Paschal Lamb and our Peace Offering, has been sacrificed for us (I Corinthians 5:7; Exodus 12:7, 13, 46; John 19:31-36). How right to trust in God whose z'roah (arm) is stretched out to save his people today as in days of old!

(All say:)

"Worthy is the Lamb who was slain to receive power and riches and wisdom, and strength and honor and glory and blessing!" (Revelation 5:12).

The egg (chagigah) recalls the festival sacrifices brought at Passover, Pentecost and Tabernacles by those, like Joseph, Mary and Jesus, who came on pilgrimage to Jerusalem to rejoice before the Lord (Deuteronomy 16:16). It is also a remembrance of the "chagigah of the 14th Nisan," another roasted lamb or kid, which in the time of Jesus was eaten at the seder before the paschal lamb. The Passover sh'lamim, peace offerings—"chagigot of the 15th Nisan"—were being sacrificed while Jesus was on the cross. These "pesachim" (John 18:28) were offered to make reconciliation for the "house of Israel" (Ezekiel 45:15, 17).

The egg is a symbol both of mourning and renewal. After a Jewish funeral the principal mourners eat an egg. We mourn for our Lord because we ourselves, Jews and

44

Gentiles, through our sins are responsible for his death. Now we rejoice before him who was resurrected; for we, dead to sin, may live forever with him.

Unleavened Bread
(Point to the matzah and say:)

This unleavened bread reminds us that the deliverance of Israel from Egypt came so swiftly—the Egyptians sent them out in haste—that there was no time for the dough to rise and become leavened (Exodus 12:33-34, 39). It was such bread that Jesus broke at the Last Supper. Its very appearance recalls the stripes and blows he bore for us. To ensure that it did not become leavened during baking, it was pierced in many places. He was pierced for us.

"Therefore purge out the old leaven, that you may be a new lump, since you truly are unleavened. For indeed Christ, our Passover, was sacrificed for us. Therefore let us keep the feast, not with old leaven, nor with the leaven of malice and wickedness, but with the unleavened bread of sincerity and truth" (I Corinthians 5:7-8).

"Jesus said . . . 'For the bread of God is He who comes down from heaven and gives life to the world. . . . I am the bread of life'" (John 6:32-35).

Bitter Herb

(Point to the bitter herb and say:)

Bitter herbs recall the bitterness of slavery in Egypt, warning us against the bitter slavery of sin; and they remind the heart burdened with its own bitterness that, not being filled with God's joy, makes the Lord a stranger. "Let all bitterness . . . be put away from you" (Ephesians 4:31). ". . . looking diligently . . . lest any root of bitterness springing up cause trouble, and by this many become defiled" (Hebrews 12:15). "But if you have bitter envy and self-seeking in your hearts, do not boast" (James 3:14).

A garden invaded by horseradish cannot be cleansed merely by cutting off the tops of the plants. Every piece of root must be eradicated. From a single root many new shoots will spring. Similarly sin within us must be uprooted, not merely "topped."

"'And I will pour on the house of David and on the inhabitants of Jerusalem the Spirit of grace and supplication; then they will look on Me whom they have pierced; they will mourn for Him as one mourns for his only son, and grieve for Him as one grieves for a firstborn. . . . In that day a fountain shall be opened . . . for sin and for uncleanness'" (Zechariah 12:10, 13:1).

(A moment or two for meditation.)

While we consider the Passover symbols, God may be speaking to us individually, asking whether we have fully and freely accepted his offer of freedom at this *Chag Haggeulah*, Festival of Redemption. Have we, for example, sprinkled metaphorically the Blood of the Lamb on the doorposts of our hearts in the face of human and spiritual opposition, clearly trusting in God to deliver us?

Now may be the time fully to receive God's gift, freely to give God his due. "'You shall love the LORD your God with all your heart, with all your soul, and with all your might'" (Deuteronomy 6:5). "'You shall worship the Lord your God, and Him only you shall serve'" (Matthew 4:10).

46

"Set my spirit free . . ." is a prayer to which we may gladly add: "Amen. Blessed art Thou." This we may do by singing the En Kelohenu, the verses of which form the acrostic *AMEN. BARUCH ATAH.*

(Sing to the tune of *En Kelohenu:*)

En Kelohenu

REMEMBERING, REDEMPTION AND REFLECTION THROUGH PRAISE

Say, "God Did It For Me!"

All bear the stamp of Adam. Yet, every one is unique; none is exactly like another. Therefore each person ought to say, "For my sake the world was created to proclaim the greatness of God" (Sanhedrin 4:5).

Likewise, everyone should think of himself or herself as having personally gone forth from Egypt, because the Word declares, "And you shall tell your son in that day, saying, 'This is done because of what the LORD did for me when I came up from Egypt'" (Exodus 13:8).

God who redeemed us from slavery in Egypt redeemed us at another Passover from the bondage of sin, so that each one of us may say, I keep this feast because of that which the Lord did for *me* when he saved me at Calvary; my old self was crucified with him, the sinful body destroyed, that I might be no longer enslaved to sin; being dead to sin, alive to God in Y'shua the Messiah. (See Romans 6:6-8, 11.)[11]

So We Praise Him
(Raise the Cup of Thanksgiving and say:)

Therefore, we are bound to thank, praise, glorify, extol and adore God who did all these wonders for our ancestors and for us. God brought us forth . . .

Celebrant	Company
From slavery	*to freedom,*
From anguish	*to joy,*
From mourning	*to festivity,*
From darkness	*to great light,*
From bondage	*to redemption.*[12]

Let us therefore sing to God a new song.

(All say:)

Hallelujah!

(Sing:)

Rejoice In The Lord Always

Hallel — Praise

(Part I — Psalms 113-114)

Psalms 113-118, collectively known as *Hallel*, were sung in the Temple while the paschal lambs were slain. After the Passover narrative we are ready to praise God with joy and thanksgiving.

The meal, an essential part of our worship, is embedded in the Hallel itself. We begin with the first two of these psalms. Then, when we eat the meal, it is not as a respite from prayer but as a reminder that God desires us to enjoy soberly *all* his bountiful gifts, not only the spiritual ones.

At the end of the meal, with its climax of eating the aphikoman and of drinking the Cup of Blessing, we conclude by rejoicing in the Hallel, Psalms 113-118. This was probably the hymn which the disciples and Jesus sang before they walked across the Kidron Valley to Gethsemane.[13]

Celebrant	Company
Blessed be the God of Israel	*Who makes us rejoice with psalms of praise.*

Psalm 113

Celebrant	Company
Praise, O servants of the LORD,	*Praise the name of the LORD!*
Blessed be the name of the LORD	*From this time forth and forevermore!*
From the rising of the sun to its going down	*The LORD's name is to be praised.*
The LORD is high above all nations,	*And His glory above the heavens.*
Who is like the LORD our God,	*Who dwells on high,*
Who humbles Himself to behold	*The things that are in the heavens and in the earth?*
He raises the poor out of the dust,	*And lifts the needy out of the ash heap,*

50

That He may seat him with princes —	*With the princes of His people.*
He grants the barren woman a home,	*Like a joyful mother of children.*

(All:)

Hallelujah!

God's humility! The Lord came down from his high place and took earthly form to raise us to heavenly places.

Psalm 114

When Israel went out of Egypt,
The house of Jacob from a people of strange
    language,
Judah became His sanctuary,[14]
And Israel His dominion.

The sea saw it and fled;
Jordan turned back.
The mountains skipped like rams,
The hills like little lambs.

What ails you, O sea, that you fled?
O Jordan, that you turned back?
O mountains, that you skipped like rams?
O hills, like little lambs?

Tremble, O earth, at the presence of the LORD,
At the presence of the God of Jacob,
Who turned the rock into a pool of water,
The flint into a fountain of waters.

The Cup Of Thanksgiving

I will deliver you from bondage

(Raise the second cup and say:)

"[Jesus] took the cup, and gave thanks, and said, 'Take this and divide it among yourselves; for I say to you, I will not drink of the fruit of the vine until the kingdom of God comes'" (Luke 22:17-18).

Blessed art Thou, O Lord our God, King of the Universe, who hast redeemed Thy people from Egypt and hast entrusted to them the oracles of God, so that Jesus, born as a Jew, be nurtured in the Scriptures that speak of him.

We thank Thee for the Passover, for the Feast of Unleavened Bread, but especially that Thou hast redeemed us to be thy children through Y'shua the Messiah, in whom we have redemption, the forgiveness of sins, through his blood.

Blessed art Thou, O Lord, Redeemer of Israel.

"'I am the true vine,'" said Jesus, "'and My Father is the vinedresser'" (John 15:1-8). May we, the branches, abide in him and bear much fruit.

Blessed art Thou, O Lord our God, King of the Universe, who createst the fruit of the vine.

בָּרוּךְ אַתָּה יְיָ אֱלֹהֵינוּ מֶלֶךְ הָעוֹלָם בּוֹרֵא פְּרִי הַגָּפֶן:

Baruch ata Adonai Elohaynu melech ha-olam boray p'ree haggafen.

(We drink.)

THE MEAL — PREPARATION, PRAYER AND PARTAKING

Rachatzah — Washing

"Wash yourselves, make yourselves clean" (Isaiah 1:16).

"Cleanse your hands, you sinners" (James 4:8).

"I will wash my hands in innocence; So I will go about Your altar, O LORD" (Psalm 26:6).

In Capernaum the disciples had been discussing somewhat heatedly their personal expectations about who was to be greatest in the kingdom of God (Matthew 18:1-4, 19:27-30; Mark 9:33-37). Soon they were to go to

Jerusalem. Later, Salome, wife of Zebedee, started them arguing again by asking Jesus to give special favors to her sons, James and John (Matthew 20:20-28; Mark 10:35-45; Luke 9:46).

Even at the Passover meal the disciples apparently were bickering over who should be regarded as greatest (Luke 22:24).[15] Y'shua's response was, "'he who is greatest among you, let him be as the younger, and he who governs as he who serves'" (Luke 22:26).

Doing the work of a servant, Jesus arose, girded himself with a towel, poured water, washed the disciples' feet, wiped them with the towel and sat down again. He said, "'You call me Teacher [Rabbi] and Lord, and you say well, for so I am. . . . I have given you an example, that you should do as I have done to you'" (John 13:13, 15).

(The Celebrant, in remembrance, washes and dries the hands or feet of some at the table. The jug and basin may be passed around so that each may wash a neighbor and be washed.)

Blessed art Thou, O Lord our God, King of the Universe, who commands us to be cleansed and to serve others; that all may lift up holy hands (I Timothy 2:8) without anger or quarreling, being at peace with one another.

בָּרוּךְ אַתָּה יְיָ אֱלֹהֵינוּ מֶלֶךְ הָעוֹלָם אֲשֶׁר
קִדְּשָׁנוּ בְּמִצְוֹתָיו וְצִוָּנוּ עַל נְטִילַת יָדָיִם:

*Baruch ata Adonai Elohaynu melech ha-olam
asher kidd'shanu b'mitsvotav v'tsivanu al n'teelat
yadayim.*

(To participate in this act of personal consecra-
tion before eating at the Lord's Table, we all say:)

AMEN

Motzee . . . Matzah —
Grace Before The Meal

Thanks For Daily Bread
and For The Bread Of Affliction

The uppermost wafer of matzah, like the one at the base,
reminds us of the manna that in the wilderness sustained
the Israelites with physical health, as our daily bread sus-
tains us. Yet man does not live by bread alone, but by
every word that proceeds from God. So together with the
bread that meets our mortal needs, we must take
Living Bread, the Word become flesh, that our lives be
maintained spiritually in health here on earth, to prepare
us for the rich life of the world to come. That Bread
enriches us in this life and prepares us to enjoy life eternal.

(Everyone receives a piece of the upper wafer,
over which we thank God for daily sustenance,
and also a piece of the remaining middle wafer,
the Bread of Affliction, the Humble Bread,
representing the Messiah. The Celebrant may
place the two pieces of matzah—each broken
into small portions—on separate plates, one passed round the table clockwise, the other in the
opposite direction. On one of the plates there
should be a small dish of salt, a pinch of which is
added by each person to the matzah when the
pieces are combined.)

55

We recall God's covenant of salt with his people: "'it is a covenant of salt forever before the LORD with you and your descendants with you'" (Numbers 18:19, cf. Leviticus 2:13). The words "with you" are there to encourage parents and children to be united in the service of God, incorruptibly throughout all generations, as members of "a chosen generation, a royal priesthood, a holy nation, His own special people," his *am segulah* (I Peter 2:9).

Jesus said: "'You are the salt of the earth'" (Matthew 5:13) and, "'have salt in yourselves, and have peace'" (Mark 9:50). He *is* our peace.

(Now we say the two blessings:)

Blessed art Thou, O Lord our God, King of the Universe, who brings forth bread from the earth.

בָּרוּךְ אַתָּה יְיָ אֱלֹהֵינוּ מֶלֶךְ הָעוֹלָם
הַמּוֹצִיא לֶחֶם מִן הָאָרֶץ

Baruch ata Adonai Elohaynu melech ha-olam hamotzee lechem min ha-aretz.

Blessed art Thou, O Lord our God, King of the Universe, who hast sanctified us by Thy commandment to eat unleavened bread.

בָּרוּךְ אַתָּה יְיָ אֱלֹהֵינוּ מֶלֶךְ הָעוֹלָם אֲשֶׁר
קִדְּשָׁנוּ בְּמִצְוֹתָיו וְצִוָּנוּ עַל אֲכִילַת מַצָּה:

Baruch ata Adonai Elohaynú melech ha-olam asher kidd'shanu b'mitzvotav v'tsivanu al acheelat matzah.

(We eat the two pieces of matzah together and say:)

Make us Thy bread, Thou who hast created us from the dust of the earth; grant us heavenly grace that we, to Thy glory, may be able to feed others with the riches of

57

Thy Word as well as with other necessities for their daily living.

MAROR   Bitter herb

(Put a piece of maror into a teaspoon of charoset and say:)

Blessed art Thou, O Lord our God, King of the Universe, who sanctifies us by Thy commandment to eat the bitter herb.

בָּרוּךְ אַתָּה יְיָ אֱלֹהֵינוּ מֶלֶךְ הָעוֹלָם אֲשֶׁר קִדְּשָׁנוּ בְּמִצְוֹתָיו וְצִוָּנוּ עַל אֲכִילַת מָרוֹר:

Baruch ata Adonai Elohaynu melech ha-olam asher kidd'shanu b'mitzvotav v'tzivanu al acheelat maror.

Korech — Sandwich

Rabbi Hillel invented it, combining matzah, bitter herb and lamb or kid. It is commonly called, "the sop."

When Jesus as a child sat learning in the Temple at Passover, one of the rabbis who was impressed by the way he listened and asked questions may have been Hillel (died A.D. 10). He established the custom of combining bitter herbs and matzah with a piece of the paschal lamb to literally fulfill the Scripture, "with unleavened bread and with bitter herbs they shall eat it" (Exodus 12:8; cf. Numbers 9:11). As the paschal lamb was the last item eaten at the seder, this combination emphasized the significance of the matzah (specifically, the aphikoman) eaten with it. Moreover, lamb being absent at the festivities outside Jerusalem, the aphikoman took on much of the mystique associated with the paschal lamb. Jesus had foretold destruction of the Temple and the consequent end of Passover sacrifices. It was realistic for him then to desire his followers to remember him in the breaking of bread in the future. The paschal sacrifice which could be offered only by dwellers in or pilgrims to Jerusalem was soon to cease. When Jerusalem fell, lamb was no longer eaten at the seder. With aphikoman alone we can remember the Lamb, our Messiah.

(We each make a sandwich of matzah — the bottom wafer — with bitter herb and possibly charoset, and we eat it without saying a special blessing.)

This portion is often given by the Celebrant to some dear one as a special mark of affection. In general, a husband will give it with love—and in wisdom—to his wife.

As they ate the chagigah, Jesus said, "'. . . one of you will betray me.'" Reclining close to his breast, a disciple (probably John) asked, "'Lord, who is it?'" "'It is he to whom I shall give a piece of bread when I have dipped it,'" replied Jesus, and gave it to Judas Iscariot. "'What you do, do quickly,'" Jesus said. (See John 13:21-27.)

When we are tempted to do wrong, the opportunity to repent is often only momentary before our hearts harden and evil takes possession of them. Had Judas seized that moment, he would have gone to the priests, saying, "I will not shed innocent blood." But allowing Satan to remain dominant within him, the most needy of the disciples received chagigah, maror and matzah, dipped as a love-token in the dish by Jesus. Immediately he went out into the dark night. Although too late after the betrayal to repent, stirred by remorse, Judas declared to the priests, "'I have sinned by betraying innocent blood'" (Matthew 27:3-4).[16]

So it seems that Judas was not present with the disciples as they ate the paschal lamb. Nor was he present as Jesus distributed the aphikoman and after supper blessed the Cup of Blessing and Redemption. Possibly Judas had arranged to partake of paschal lamb with the Temple officers whom he led afterwards to Gethsemane.

Jesus had showed his erring disciple that he still loved him. This action reinforced his previous reply to Peter's question, "'How often shall my brother sin against me, and I forgive him?'" (Matthew 18:21-35). It also illustrated his commands, "love one another" (John 15:12), "love your enemies . . . do good to those who hate you, and pray for those who spitefully use you" (Matthew 5:44).

SHULCHAN ORECH   Table set for meal

Agape

(As the meal reaches its climax.)

We prepare to come close to the Lord at his table.

The table in one's home, or wherever we are assembled together in God's name, takes the place of the altar that once stood in the sanctuary. This, at which we now sit, is the table before the Lord (Ezekiel 41:22).

When the Lord's friends meet, they have the opportunity of seeing God in each other's eyes and in selfless fellowship.

Who are the Lord's friends?

"'You are My friends,'" said Jesus, "'if you do whatever I command you'" (John 15:14). "'This is My commandment, that you LOVE ONE ANOTHER AS I HAVE LOVED YOU'" (John 15:12, emphasis ours).

"'A new commandment I give to you, that you love one another; as I have loved you, that you also love one another. By this all will know that you are My disciples, if you have love for one another'" (John 13:34-35).

HOW OFTEN WE HAVE FAILED GOD!

Jesus knocks on the door; we have to open.
Sometimes he seems hidden; we have to search.
He provides a lamp for our feet;
the illumination avails nothing,
if we do not walk with him.

"'While you have the light, believe in the light, that you may become sons of light.' These things Jesus spoke, and departed, and was hidden from them" (John 12:36).

Jesus was hidden from the people; they did not believe. Some who did believe, did not confess it out of fear. "Nevertheless even among the rulers many believed in Him, but because of the Pharisees they did not confess Him, lest they should be put out of the synagogue; for they loved the praise of men more than the praise of God" (John 12:42-43).

Tsaphoon — Hidden

(The aphikoman is searched for and found. The cloth in which it has been wrapped is placed before the Celebrant. Fill the third cup, the Cup of Blessing and Redemption.)

(The Celebrant takes the aphikoman from its wrapping and says:)

"'For this commandment which I command you today, it is not too mysterious [hidden] for you, nor is it far off. It is not in heaven . . . Nor is it beyond the sea . . . But the word is very near you, in your mouth and in your heart, that you may do it'" (Deuteronomy 30:11-14). May we do the will of our Father in heaven, who gives us the Heavenly Bread that once was hidden, but now is revealed.

A Grace Of Thanksgiving

N'varech—Let us bless the Lord. Those who seek the Lord shall not lack any good thing. Blessed is the one who trusts the Lord. The Lord will give strength to his people; the Lord will bless his people with peace (wholeness). (Psalms 34:10, 40:4, 29:11)

(Company recites:)

Baruch haggever asher yivtach b'Adonai
v'ha-ya Adonai mivtacho.
Adonai oz l'ammo yitten
Adonai y'varech et ammo bashalom. C

(Celebrant, taking the aphikoman, says:)

The night he was delivered up, Jesus took bread and gave thanks.

(Company:)

Blessed art Thou, O Lord our God, King of the Universe, who feedest the whole world with goodness, grace, lovingkindness and tender mercy; who givest bread to all flesh, for Thy lovingkindness is ever enduring.

Blessed be God our Father, who promised to send his people Israel a Redeemer to plead their cause, to make an end to sin, to make reconciliation for iniquity and to bring in everlasting righteousness by anointing the Most Holy, our Redeemer and Savior, Amen. 17

(Celebrant:)

Our Father, we thank you for sending us Jesus the Messiah, Y'shua ha-Mashiach, who broke bread

(Break the aphikoman.)

and gave it to his disciples.

(Distribute the pieces on a plate to the company.)

He said to them, " 'Take, eat, *Zeh guphee han-nittan b'adchem;* this is my body which is given for you. Do this in remembrance of Me' " (Mark 14:22; Luke 22:19).[18]

Feed on him in your hearts by faith with thanksgiving.

(All eat, and say:)

"Thanks be to God for His indescribable gift!" (II Corinthians 9:15)

(Nothing further is eaten at the seder after this.)

(Keep silence awhile; then sing:)

Bind Us Together

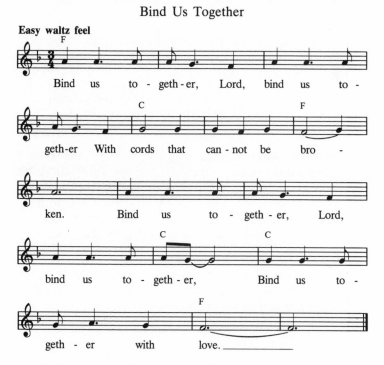

(Celebrant:)

The God of all the families of Israel has declared:
"'I have loved you with an everlasting love . . .'"
(Jeremiah 31:3b). God's love has been poured into our
hearts. Therefore let us love the Lord our God with heart,
soul and might, and love one another as Y'shua has
commanded.

The Peace

The peace of the Lord be always with you and between
us. *Shalom alaychem.*

THE CUP OF BLESSING AND REDEMPTION

("I will redeem you with an outstretched arm.")

After the meal, lest the Redeemer be forgotten, Jesus took
the Cup of Blessing, recalling the third of God's promises
to enslaved Israel.

(Raise the third cup and say:)

Reaffirming what he had said over the cup before
supper, Jesus declared, "'But I say to you, I will not drink
of this fruit of the vine from now on until that day when I
drink it new with you in My Father's kingdom'"
(Matthew 26:29).

And with authority he said to them, "*Zeh Damee,
Dam habb'rit hachadashah hannishpach b'ad rabbim.*"
"'For this is My blood of the new covenant, which is shed
for many for the remission of sins'" (Matthew 26:28).[19]
"'This cup is the new covenant in My blood. This do, as
often as you drink it, in remembrance of Me'"
(I Corinthians 11:25).

64

Giving thanks, the Messiah said:

(All:)

Blessed art Thou, O Lord our God, King of the Universe, who createst the fruit of the vine.

בָּרוּךְ אַתָּה יְיָ אֱלֹהֵינוּ מֶלֶךְ הָעוֹלָם בּוֹרֵא פְּרִי
הַגָּפֶן:

Baruch ata Adonai Elohaynu melech ha-olam boray p'ree haggafen.

I will lift up the cup of salvation (Y'shua) and call on the Lord's name.

(Celebrant:)

Remember that Y'shua's blood was shed for us to preserve us for everlasting life. Let us be thankful.

(We drink the third cup.)

"For as often as you eat this bread and drink this cup, you proclaim[20] the Lord's death till He comes" (I Corinthians 11:26). "The cup of blessing which we bless, is it not the communion of the blood of Christ? The bread which we break, is it not the communion of the body of Christ?" (I Corinthians 10:16)

We have partaken of the aphikoman, remembering the One who was to come, has already come and will come again.

Christian and Jew have a belief in common, yet with this difference: The Torah-true Jew believes the Messiah is to come; the Torah-based Christian, that he is to come again.

(Fill the fourth cup—the Cup of Completion.
Fill also a fifth cup, from which we shall not drink.)

THE FIFTH CUP — CUP OF ELIJAH

Rooted in the belief that Elijah comes to proclaim the Messiah's advent (Malachi 4:5) and Israel's restoration, the legend that Elijah visits every Jewish home at Passover has flourished. Families open their doors for him (often setting a special place for him at the table), and children closely examine Elijah's cup, sure that he has sipped the wine!

For centuries Jews in many lands have been afraid to open their doors at Passover-Easter time for fear of reprisals from so-called Christians, e.g., the riots at York on Passover Eve (1190) and in Russia during Easter (1881-1905). Even in our 20th Century some, both Jews and Gentiles, fear a knock on their doors because of the violence of ungodly people.

Committed Christians are often too shy to tell non-believing friends who are in spiritual or physical need the good news that wholeness is available for the asking. What we know to be evil is frequently advocated in society as good. Often, those who seek to do good like Jesus are dubbed (as if they were evil-doers) "do-gooders." Yet God has made us guardians of his truth. So every night must be for us, as it was for Israel on the eve of the Exodus, "a night of solemn observance" (Exodus 12:42).[21]

On the first day of the week[22] (after the crucifixion), when the doors were shut where the disciples were assembled, for fear of the Jews (actually Judeans),[23] Jesus came and stood in their midst, and said to them, "'Shalom alaychem[24] — Peace be with you'" (John 20:19).

We know, indeed, who stands at the door of our hearts and homes. "'Behold, I stand at the door and knock. If any one hears my voice and opens the door, I will come in to him and dine with him, and he with Me'" (Revelation 3:20).

(Company sings:)

Behold I Stand At The Door And Knock

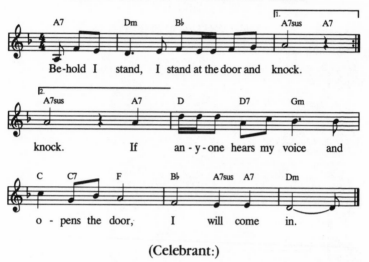

Be-hold I stand, I stand at the door and knock.

knock. If an - y - one hears my voice and

o - pens the door, I will come in.

(Celebrant:)

I will come in to him and will sup with him and he with me.

(Company:)

Blessed art Thou, O Lord our God, King of the Universe, who stretches out the heavens, lays the foundation of the earth and forms the spirit of man within him (Zechariah 12:1).

בָּרוּךְ אַתָּה יְיָ אֱלֹהֵינוּ מֶלֶךְ הָעוֹלָם נֹטֶה שָׁמַיִם
וְיֹסֵד אָרֶץ וְיֹצֵר רוּחַ-אָדָם בְּקִרְבּוֹ׃

Baruch ata Adonai Elohaynu melech ha-olam noteh shama-yim v'yosed aretz v'yotzayr ru-ach adam b'keerbo.

We open the door in faith,[25] praying in the words of the prophet Joel:

Pour out Thy Spirit upon all flesh as Thou hast promised, O Lord, that our sons and our daughters may prophesy, our old men dream dreams and young men see

68

visions. And also, upon Thy menservants and maidservants, pour out Thy Spirit as Thou hast said. (See Joel 2:28-29.)

(Sing:)

Spirit Of The Living God

Slowly with expression

Spir - it of the liv - ing God, fall a - fresh on me; Spir - it of the liv - ing God, fall a - fresh on me. Break me, melt me, mold me, fill me! Spir - it of the liv - ing God, fall a - fresh on me.

Spirit Of The Living God, by Daniel Iverson
© Copyright 1935, 1963. Moody Press.
Moody Bible Institute of Chicago. Used by permission.

"But let all those rejoice who put their trust in You; let them ever shout for joy, because You defend them; let those also who love Your name be joyful in You" (Psalm 5:11).

"But to you who fear My name the Sun of Righteousness shall arise with healing in His wings" (Malachi 4:2).

(The door is closed.)

Hallel: Scripture and Song

When they had sung a hymn, Jesus went out to the Mount of Olives as was his custom, over the Kidron Valley, where there was a garden in a place called Gethsemane, which he and his disciples entered (synthesis of Matthew 26:30, 36; Mark 14:26, 32; Luke 22:39; John 18:1).

The hymn they sang could have been the latter part of the Hallel.

(Either Hallel or Nishmat, or both, may be said here.)

Hallel Part II — Psalms 115-118, abridged

Psalm 115

Celebrant: Not unto us, O Lord, not unto us, but to Your name give glory,

Company: *Because of Your mercy, and because of Your truth.*

Celebrant: The Lord has been mindful of us; He will bless us.

Company: *He will bless those who fear the Lord, both small and great.*

Celebrant: But we will bless the Lord from this time forth and forevermore.

Company: *Praise the Lord!*

Psalm 116-117

Celebrant: I love the Lord, who has heard my voice and my supplications.

Company: *Because He has inclined His ear to me, therefore I will call upon the Lord as long as I live.*

Celebrant: Return to your rest, O my soul, for the Lord has dealt bountifully with you.

Company: *What shall I render to the Lord for all His benefits toward me?*

Celebrant: I will take up the cup of salvation, and call upon the name of the Lord.

Company: *I will offer to You the sacrifice of thanksgiving. Praise the Lord!*

Celebrant: Oh, praise the Lord, all you Gentiles! Laud Him, all you peoples.

Company: *For His merciful kindness is great toward us, and the truth of the Lord endures forever. Praise the Lord!*

(Company sings:)

Eternally Grateful

I am e - ter - nal-ly grate - ful to Je - sus for all he has done for me. He has giv - en me life and sal - va - tion Giv - en me lib - er - ty Oh Lord I praise and I___ bless your name. Give the glo - ry to you to you my

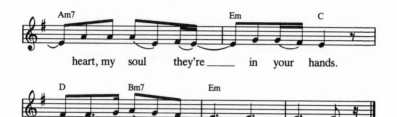

heart, my soul they're ____ in your hands.

Teach me to wor - ship you. ____

2. I will lift up the cup of salvation and
   Call upon his name
   Through his blood I have redemption
   A brand new life I claim.

3. Bless the Lord, bless the Lord, O my soul
   And all that's within my frame
   Join and sing out the praises of Jesus
   Eternal forever the same.

Psalm 118

Celebrant: Oh, give thanks to the Lord, for He is good!
Hodu l'adonai kee tov.

Company: *Because His mercy endures forever.*
Kee l'olam chasdo.

Celebrant: Let those who fear the Lord now say,

Company: *"His mercy endures forever."*
Kee l'olam chasdo.

Celebrant: I called on the Lord in distress; the Lord
answered me and set me in a broad place.

Company: *The Lord is on my side; I will not fear.*
What can man do to me?

Celebrant: The Lord is my strength and song, and He
has become my salvation.

Company: *The stone which the builders rejected has*
become the chief cornerstone.

Celebrant: This was the Lord's doing; it is marvelous in
our eyes.

(Company sings:)

Come And Praise The Lord

73

In my trouble I asked him to save me;
He answered and set me in safety.

(Chorus)

The Lord my redeemer is for me;
No more can the wicked destroy me.

(Chorus)

The stone which the builders rejected
The Lord has made the cornerstone for all.

(Chorus)

Celebrant: *Hoshee-a na!* Save now, I pray, O Lord. [26]

Company: *O Lord, I pray, send now prosperity.*

Celebrant: Blessed is he who comes in the name of the Lord![27]

Company: *The Lord is God and He has given us light.*

Celebrant: We bless you from the house of the Lord.

Company: *Hoshee-a na! Save now, I pray, O Lord.*

Celebrant: You are my God, and I will praise You;

Company: *You are my God, I will exalt You.*

Celebrant: Oh, give thanks to the Lord, for He is good!
Hodu l'Adonai kee tov.

Company: *For his mercy endures forever.*
Kee l'olam chasdo.
All Your works shall praise You, O Lord.
It is good to give thanks, and right to praise
Your name.
From everlasting to everlasting,
You are God.
Hallelujah. Amen.

Nishmat Kol Chai — The Blessing Of Song

A Jewish—not a Christian—tradition of medieval or earlier date, current in France and Germany, ascribes the composition of this ancient prayer to Simeon Caipha (Aramaic for Simon Peter). Who knows whether or not Peter did compose it? Certainly it is one of the most beautiful prayers in the Jewish liturgy. "Blessing of Song" (*Birkat Hashir*) is the title given it in the Talmud (Pesachim 118a).

(Celebrant:)

Nishmat kol chai t-varech et-shim'cha Adonai Elohaynu. . . .

The breath of every living creature blesses Thy name, O Lord our God. The spirit of all flesh continuously glorifies and exalts Thy remembrance, O our King. From everlasting throughout eternity Thou art God. Besides Thee we have neither king, redeemer nor savior, freeing and delivering, upholding and showing tender mercy at all times of trouble and distress. Indeed, we have no king but Thee.

God before the beginning of time and beyond the end, God of all creatures, Lord of all generations, lauded with a wealth of praises, guiding the world with lovingkindness and all creatures with tender mercy. The Lord neither sleeps nor slumbers. God awakens sleepers, rouses slumberers, gives speech to the dumb, sets free bound prisoners, supports the falling and raises those who are bowed down. To Thee alone we give thanks.

(Company:)[28]

Were our mouths full of song as the sea
Our tongues with joy as its many waves,
Our lips with praise as the breadth of the sky;
Though our eyes shone with light as the sun and
the moon,
Our hands outspread as the eagles of heaven,
And we—like gazelles—were swift of foot,

We still could not thank Thee, nor bless Thy
  name,
For even one thousandth of the many thousands,
Or one ten-thousandth of innumerable myriads
Of the goodly gifts which Thou hast given
In the past to our ancestors and now to us.

Yet the limbs which Thou hast shaped in us,
The spirit and soul Thou has breathed into us,
The tongue which Thou hast put in our mouths,
Shall thank and bless, extol and give glory,
Exalt and reverence, hallow and do homage
Unto Thy name, O Lord our King.

Each mouth to Thee gives thanks,
To Thee all tongues must swear;
All knees shall bend to Thee,
All bow in love and fear.

(Celebrant:)

Every bone in my body shall cry,
"My Lord! Who is like unto Thee?"

THE CUP OF COMPLETION

Jesus had said, "'I will no longer drink of the fruit of the vine until that day when I drink it new in the kingdom of God'" (Mark 14:25). Let us think of him now at Gethsemane, praying alone from his sleepy disciples, saying as he knelt, "'Father, if it is Your will, remove this cup from Me; nevertheless not My will, but Yours, be done'" (Luke 22:42, Mark 14:36). An angel appeared, strengthening him. Still he agonized, his sweat like great drops of blood falling to the ground (Luke 22:43-44). Finally, the ordeal was accepted, victory won. Later, when soldiers came for him, he would say, "'Shall I not drink the cup which My Father has given Me?'" (John 18:11). At Calvary, atonement (*kapporah*) was made.

Then Judas appeared with a band of Temple police supported by Roman soldiers. With a kiss he betrayed. When Jesus then pronounced the ineffable name of God ("'I am He.'" John 18:5-6), all fell to the ground. Jesus had power to escape, but submitted to arrest and was bound and interrogated. At the prompting of the chief priests he was brought the next day before Pontius Pilate, who was unwilling to face the one who is truth. Pilate was guilty of murder and treason against one whom he should have acknowledged as his king. Having declared Y'shua innocent, he had him flogged and crucified as a criminal. The dramatic gesture of washing his hands actually did nothing to cleanse Pilate.

Before crucifixion, Jesus refused wine mingled with myrrh which was given him to drink (Mark 15:23). On the cross, towards the end, Jesus cried, "'I thirst!'" With a sprig of hyssop, which can serve as a reminder that the blood of Jesus cleanses us from all sin (I John 1:7, cf. Exodus 12:21-23) a sponge filled with sour wine was put to his mouth. Jesus who had refused wine now received it (John 19:28-30, cf. Luke 22:18). His work of atonement completed, he cried, "'It is finished!'" (Greek: Tetelestai; Hebrew: Neshlam) and commended his spirit into the hands of the Father.

Y'shua breathed his last. The Lord of the Sabbath rested on the sabbath. He rose on the first day of the week. He lives again and is alive today!

בּוֹרֵא פְּרִי הַגָּפֶן

The Cup Of Completion,
Of Sorrow, Death and Victory

(All lift the fourth cup and say:)

"I will take you as My people, and I will be your God" (Exodus 6:7).

(We bless again with the blessing
that has been on Jesus' lips:)

Blessed art Thou, O Lord our God, King of the Universe, who createst the fruit of the vine.

בָּרוּךְ אַתָּה יְיָ אֱלֹהֵינוּ מֶלֶךְ הָעוֹלָם בּוֹרֵא פְּרִי
הַגָּפֶן:

Baruch ata Adonai Elohaynu melech ha-olam boray p'ree haggafen.

(Drink.)

Neertzah — Acceptance

The paschal seder is done,
Its customs and laws fulfilled;
Grant grace that we, each one,
May do as Thou hast willed.

O pure One, enthroned above,
Raise up the low, make free;
Replant on Zion in love
Thy vine-branch, nigh to Thee.

Fulfill, O Lord, the desires and requests of Thy servants as is best for us; and grant us in this world knowledge of Thy truth, and in the world to come, life everlasting.

"And He said to me, 'It is done! I am the Alpha and the Omega, the Beginning and the End. I will give of the fountain of the water of life freely to him who thirsts. He who overcomes shall inherit all things, and I will be his God and he shall be My son.'" (Revelation 21:6-7)

Again we remember God's promise in Jeremiah 31:33: "'But this is the covenant that I will make with the house of Israel after those days, says the LORD: I will put My law in their minds, and write it on their hearts; and I will be their God, and they shall be My people.'" (See also Exodus 6:7.)

L'shanah Haba-ah Bi-yerushala-yim Habb'nu-yah Uv'yamaynu B'zo Hachadashah

Next year in Jerusalem built anew
And in our days the New Jerusalem.

"And I saw a new heaven and a new earth, for the first heaven and the first earth had passed away. Also there was no more sea. Then I, John, saw the holy city, New Jerusalem, coming down out of heaven from God, prepared as a bride adorned for her husband. And I heard a loud voice from heaven saying, 'Behold, the tabernacle of God is with men, and He will dwell with them, and they shall be His people, and God Himself will be with them and be their God. And God will wipe away every tear from their eyes; there shall be no more death, nor sorrow, nor crying; and there shall be no more pain, for the former things have passed away'" (Revelation 21:1-4).

PART III

PSALMS FOR PESACH

PART III

A

MESSIANIC

CELEBRATION

ברך

v.1: sing once (no repeat)
vv.2,3,4: sing twice
v.5: sing three times

1. Ad - dir Hu____ Blest_ is He____
2. Chas - sid Hu De - liv - er - er He E -
ter - nal Faith - ful Gra - cious He

Swift - ly come in glo - ry Speed thy_ ways to
Great His love and mer - cy. He who a - based his

show thy face. Haste to build thy Ho - ly place.
cho - sen face. Quick - ly par - dons their dis-grace.

Build, re - new for thy prom - is - es are true.

Build Jer - u - sa - lem the New.

Hadur Hu—Honored is He

3. *Hadur Hu,* Infinite He,
Just, King, Lord and Merciful He
Comforter and Savior;
The Son still pleads His people's case
Wins them favor, blessing, grace.
Build, renew. . .

Na'or Hu—Tremendous is He

4. *Na'or Hu,* Ordainer He,
Physician, Quickener, Redeemer, He
Longs for our returning;
Sin and ill He shall efface,
Heavenly joys our tears replace.
Build renew. . .

Sagiv Hu—Uplifted is He

5. *Sagiv Hu,* True is He,
   Unchangeable, Victor, Worshipful He,
   Exalted, yea the Zenith He,
   Yet there is none nearer!
   So to Him who all our days
   Cares for, guides us, offer praise.
   Build, renew, for Thy promises are true,
   Build Jerusalem the New.

KEE LO NA-EH, KEE LO YA-EH [30]
BECAUSE FOR HIM IT IS SEEMLY,
FOR HIM IT IS MEET

With Joy

A - dir bim - 'loo - chah ba - choor ka - ha -
la - chah, G'doo - dav yom 'roo lo: L' -
cha - u - l' - cha L' - cha kee l' - cha L' -
cha af l' - cha L' - cha A - do - nai
ha - mam - l' - cha Kee lo na - eh, Kee lo ya - eh.

Chorus: *L'cha ul'cha*
L'cha kee l'cha
L'cha af l'cha
L'cha Adonai hamam'lachah
Kee lo na-eh,
Kee lo ya-eh.

2. *Dagool bim'loochah, hadoor kahalachah,*
V'teekav yom'roo lo:
(Chorus)

3. *Zakkai bim'loochah, chaseen kahalachah,*
Taf'serav yom'roo lo:
(Chorus)

4. *Yacheed bim'loochah, kabbeer kahalachah,*
Leemoodav yom'roo lo:
(Chorus)

5. *Moshel bim'loochah, nora kahalachah,*
S'veevav yom'roo lo:
(Chorus)

6. *Anav bim'loochah, podeh kahalachah,*
Tzadeekav yom'roo lo:
(Chorus)

7. *Kadosh bim'loochah, rachoom kahalachah,*
Shin'anav yom'roo lo:
(Chorus)

8. *Takeef bim'loochah, tomeich kahalachah,*
T'meemav yom'roo lo:
(Chorus)

(And in English we sing:)

1. Mighty in royalty, chosen of right
—His legions say to Him:
   Chorus: To Thee, yea, to Thee;
   To Thee, surely to Thee;
   To Thee, truly to Thee;
   To Thee, O Lord, kingship belongeth.
   Because for Him it is seemly,
   For Him it is meet.

2. Distinguished in royalty, glorious of right,
—His faithful say to Him:

(Chorus)

3. Pure in royalty, firm of right,
—His courtiers say to Him:
(Chorus)

4. Single in royalty, mighty of right,
—His adepts say to Him:
(Chorus)

5. Ruling in royalty, feared of right,
—His surrounders say to Him:
(Chorus)

6. Humble in royalty, redeeming of right,
—His just ones say to Him:
(Chorus)

7. Holy in royalty, merciful of right,
—His angels say to Him:
(Chorus)

8. Powerful in royalty, sustaining of right,
—His innocent say to Him:
(Chorus)

ECHAD MEE YODE'A? (WHO KNOWS ONE?) [31]

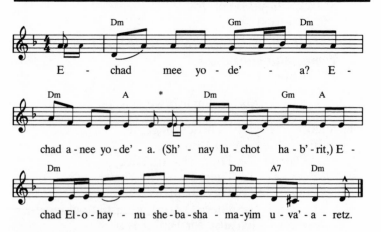

E - chad mee yo - de' - a? E - chad a - nee yo - de' - a. (Sh' - nay lu - chot ha - b' - rit,) E - chad El - o - hay - nu she - ba - sha - ma - yim u - va' - a - retz.

*Omit this phrase on 1st verse only. Sing once for each
succeeding verse, cumulatively in descending order,
in a manner reminiscent of *The Twelve Days of Christmas.*

90

2. *Sh'nayim mee yode'a?*   *Sh'nayim anee yode'a.*
   Sh'nay luchot ha-brit,
   Echad Elohay-nu shebashamayim uva'aretz.

3. *Sh'loshah mee yode'a?*   *Sh'loshah anee yode'a.*
   Sh'loshah a-vot, Sh'nay luchot ha-brit,
   Echad Elohay-nu shebashamayim uva'aretz.

4. *Arba mee yode'a?*   *Arba anee yode'a.*
   Arba eemahot, Sh'loshah a-vot, Sh'nay luchot ha-brit,
   Echad Elohay-nu shebashamayim uva'aretz.

5. *Chamishah mee yode'a?*   *Chamishah anee yode'a.*
   Chamishah chum'shay To-rah, Arba eemahot,
   Sh'loshah a-vot, Sh'nay luchot ha-brit,
   Echad Elohay-nu shebashamayim uva'aretz.

6. *Shishah mee yode'a?*   *Shishah anee yode'a.*
   Shishah sidray Mish-nah,
   Chamishah chum'shay To-rah, Arba eemahot,
   Sh'loshah a-vot, Sh'nay luchot ha-brit,
   Echad Elohay-nu shebashamayim uva'aretz.

7. *Shiv'ah mee yode'a?*   *Shiv'ah anee yode'a.*
   Shiv'ah y'may shabbatta,
   Shishah sidray Mish-nah,
   Chamishah chum'shay To-rah, Arba eemahot,
   Sh'loshah a-vot, Sh'nay luchot ha-brit,
   Echad Elohay-nu shebashamayim uva'aretz.

8. *Sh'monah mee yode'a?*   *Sh'monah anee yode'a.*
   Sh'monah y'may mee-lah,
   Shiv'ah y'may shabbatta,
   Shishah sidray Mish-nah,
   Chamishah chum'shay To-rah, Arba eemahot,
   Sh'loshah a-vot, Sh'nay luchot ha-brit,
   Echad Elohay-nu shebashamayim uva'aretz.

9. *Tish'ah mee yode'a?*   *Tish'ah anee yode'a.*
   Tish'ah yarchay lei-dah,
   Sh'monah y'may mee-lah,
   Shiv'ah y'may shabbatta,
   Shishah sidray Mish-nah,
   Chamishah chum'shay To-rah, Arba eemahot,
   Sh'loshah a-vot, Sh'nay luchot ha-brit,
   Echad Elohay-nu shebashamayim uva'aretz.

10. *Asarah mee yode'a?*   *Asarah anee yode'a.*
    Asarah dibra-ya,
    Tish'ah yarchay lei-dah,
    Sh'monah y'may mee-lah,
    Shiv'ah y'may shabbatta,
    Shishah sidray Mish-nah,
    Chamishah chum'shay **To-rah,** *Arba eemahot,*
    Sh'loshah a-vot, Sh'nay luchot ha-brit,
    Echad Elohay-nu shebashamayim uva'aretz.

11. *Achad-asar mee yode'a?* *Achad-asar anee yode'a.*
    Achad-asar coch'va-ya,
    Asarah dibra-ya,
    Tish'ah yarchay lei-dah,
    Sh'monah y'may mee-lah,
    Shiv'ah y'may shabbatta,
    Shishah sidray Mish-nah,
    Chamishah chum'shay **To-rah,** *Arba eemahot,*
    Sh'loshah a-vot, Sh'nay luchot ha-brit,
    Echad Elohay-nu shebashamayim uva'aretz.

12. *Sh'naym-asar mee*   *Sh'naym-asar anee*
    yode'a?   *yode'a.*
    Sh'naym-asar shiv'ta-ya,
    Achad-asar coch'va-ya,
    Asarah dibra-ya,
    Tish'ah yarchay lei-dah,
    Sh'monah y'may mee-lah,
    Shiv'ah y'may shabbatta,
    Shishah sidray Mish-nah,
    Chamishah chum'shay **To-rah,** *Arba eemahot,*
    Sh'loshah a-vot, Sh'nay luchot ha-brit,
    Echad Elohay-nu shebashamayim uva'aretz.

13. *Sh'loshah-asar mee*   *Sh'loshah-asar anee*
    yode'a?   *yode'a.*
    Sh'loshah-asar midaya,
    Sh'naym-asar shiv'ta-ya,
    Achad-asar coch'va-ya,
    Asarah dibra-ya,
    Tish'ah yarchay lei-dah,
    Sh'monah y'may mee-lah,
    Shiv'ah y'may shabbatta,

Shishah sidray Mish-nah,
Chamishah chum'shay To-rah, Arba eemahot,
Sh'loshah a-vot, Sh'nay luchot ha-brit,
Echad Elohay-nu shebashamayim uva'aretz.

(And in English we sing:)

Who knows one?   I know one.
One is our God in the heavens and the earth.

Who knows two?   I know two.
Two are the tables of the covenant; one is our God in the heavens and the earth.

Who knows three?   I know three.
Three are the fathers; two are the tables of the covenant; one is our God in the heavens and the earth.

Who knows four?   I know four.
Four are the mothers; three are the fathers; two are the tables of the covenant; one is our God in the heavens and the earth.

Who knows five?   I know five.
Five are the books of the Torah; four are the mothers; three are the fathers; two are the tables of the covenant; one is our God in the heavens and the earth.

Who knows six?   I know six.
Six are the orders of the Mishnah; five are the books of the Torah; four are the mothers; three are the fathers; two are the tables of the covenant; one is our God in the heavens and the earth.

Who knows seven?   I know seven.
Seven are the days of the Sabbath-count; six are the orders of the Mishnah; five are the books of the Torah; four are the mothers; three are the fathers; two are the tables of the covenant; one is our God in the heavens and the earth.

Who knows eight?   I know eight.
Eight are the days of the circumcision; seven are the days of the Sabbath-count; six are the orders of the Mishnah; five are the books of the Torah; four are the mothers; three are the fathers; two are the tables of the covenant; one is our God in the heavens and the earth.

Who knows nine?   I know nine.
Nine are the months of pregnancy; eight are the days of the circumcision; seven are the days of the Sabbath-count; six are the orders of the Mishnah; five are the books of the Torah; four are the mothers; three are the fathers; two are the tables of the covenant; one is our God in the heavens and the earth.

Who knows ten?   I know ten.
Ten are the commandments; nine are the months of pregnancy; eight are the days of the circumcision; seven are the days of the Sabbath-count; six are the orders of the Mishnah; five are the books of the Torah; four are the mothers; three are the fathers; two are the tables of the covenant; one is our God in the heavens and the earth.

Who knows eleven?   I know eleven.
Eleven are the stars of Joseph's dream; ten are the commandments; nine are the months of pregnancy; eight are the days of the circumcision; seven are the days of the Sabbath-count; six are the orders of the Mishnah; five are the books of the Torah; four are the mothers; three are the fathers; two are the tables of the covenant; one is our God in the heavens and the earth.

Who knows twelve?   I know twelve.
Twelve are the tribes of Israel; eleven are the stars of Joseph's dream; ten are the commandments; nine are the months of pregnancy; eight are the days of the circumcision; seven are the days of the Sabbath-count; six are the orders of the Mishnah; five are the books of the Torah; four are the mothers; three are the fathers; two are the tables of the covenant; one is our God in the heavens and the earth.

Who knows thirteen?   I know thirteen.
Thirteen are the attributes of Divinity; twelve are the tribes of Israel; eleven are the stars of Joseph's dream; ten are the commandments; nine are the months of pregnancy; eight are the days of the circumcision; seven are the days of the Sabbath-count; six are the orders of the Mishnah; five are the books of the Torah; four are the mothers; three are the fathers; two are the tables of the covenant; one is our God in the heavens and the earth.

HAVAH NAGEELAH:
COME, LET US PRAISE HIM^J

Come, let us praise him, Come, let us raise our
voice and re - joice Je - sus is Lord.
Come, let us praise him, Come, let us raise our
voice and re - joice Je - sus is Lord.
Let us all sing to Him, Come, let us bring to Him
Hearts ad - o - ra - tion, Grate-ful - ly out-poured.
He is the Might-y One, He is the Fath-er's son,
He reigns the on - ly one, ev - er a-dored. Wake, wake,
wake my bro - thers; Wake my bro-thers hearts a - glow-ing,

Now pre-pare the fields for sow-ing We shall see the

green shoots grow-ing, Then the gol - den har-vest grow-ing

Grain to be stored! Praise to the Lord! His mer-cies are ov-er flow-ing!

Havah nageelah, havah nageelah
Havah hageelah, v'-nis-m'cha

(Repeat)

Havah n'ran'nah, havah n'ran'nah
Havah n'ran'nah, v-nis-m'cha

(Repeat)

Uru uru achim,
Uru achim b'lev samay-ach (four times)
Uru achim uru achim b'lev samay-ach.

(Tune: Leoni—"The God of Abraham Praise")

With thank-ful-ness and joy Thy praise, O Lord, we sing;

With con-fi-dence our hearts in-to Thy pre-sence

bring. For all the bless-ed years that

we have known Thy love, As-sur-ance of a-

ton-ing pow'r our lives should prove.

2. Thy people once enslaved, from bondage then made free,
   From Egypt's land by Mighty Hand passed through the sea.
   Another Lamb was slain, a greater wonder wrought,
   Thy people with Messiah's blood by thee were bought.

3. The remnant of Thy flock, who love Messiah's name,
   Rejoicing in His gracious gift, this truth proclaim:
   Salvation through His blood-free gift to all He gave—
   Forgiveness, if men but believe His power to save.

4. The centuries have borne good fruit upon Thy Vine;
   We thank Thee for so many souls by grace made Thine.
   May all of Abraham's seed turn yearning soon to thee
   And put their trust in Him who saved at Calvary.

5. The day will surely come when all who do not see
   Thou art the One our fathers sought shall look to Thee.
   Be gracious then, we pray, to Israel's ancient race;
   Renew all hearts to serve in truth the God of Grace.

HYMN FOR THE SON OF DAVID, BOTH SHEPHERD AND LAMB

Passover is the festival of the Good shepherd, the Lamb of God. He is both our Redeemer and our Ransom. This Passover hymn is based on Psalm 23, much loved by my dear father, the Reverend Solomon Lipson, to whose memory it is dedicated. His tuneful, happy *sedarim* are recalled with joy.

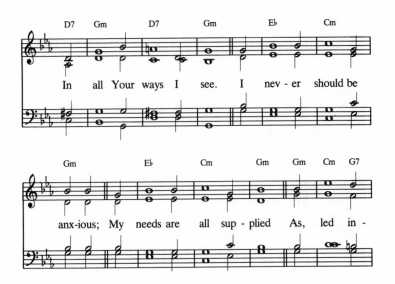

In all Your ways I see. I nev-er should be anx-ious; My needs are all sup-plied As, led in-

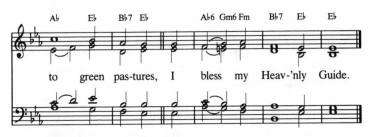

to green pas-tures, I bless my Heav-'nly Guide.

(Tune: Penlan)

2. Your crook prevents me straying,
   You do with staff protect
   And lead me on to give me
   More joys than I expect.
   In darkness when enshrouded,
   I fear no ill at all;
   Although my path be clouded,
   You never let me fall.

3. If wounded when I'm willful,
   I turn to You for aid;
   My head is soothed with oil,
   I rest within Your shade.
   Then surely I must trust You
   From whom all good things come,
   That at the end my dwelling
   Shall be Your heavenly home.

99

VA-Y'HEE BÁCHATZEE HALLAILAH —
AND IT CAME TO PASS AT MIDNIGHT[33]

In days of old great miracles were done ..... at night,
Before the early watch had scarce begun ..... at night,
Abraham's three-fold host a victory won ..... at night.
    And it came to pass at midnight.

The sins of Gerar's king were judged in a
    dream ..... at night.
The Syrian trickster, Laban, feared to scheme ..... at night.
When Jacob fought the Angel he prevailed ..... at night.
    And it came to pass at midnight.

The firstborn sons of Egypt, smitten, died ..... at night;
The Egyptians rose and missed their strength
    and pride ..... at night.
The stars in their paths against Sisera were
    allied ..... at night.
    And it came to pass at midnight.

Sennacherib's host by the angel of death was
    devoured ..... at night.
Bel and his gruesome image were overpowered ..... at night,
But Daniel the prophet with mystic vision
    was endowed ..... at night.
    And it came to pass at midnight.

Belshazzar drinking from holy cups was slain ..... at night.
Daniel was saved from lions. The dream he
    could explain ..... at night,
And Haman wrote his letters of hate in vain ..... at night.
    And it came to pass at midnight.

For when the king was sleepless he heard of
    the plot ..... at night.
O Winepresser, tread on him who asketh,
    "What ..... of the night?"
The watchman soon will say, "Tis morn
    and not ..... the night."
    And it came to pass at midnight.

Bring near the day that's neither day ..... nor night.
Most High, make known that over light is
    Thy sway ..... as over night;

Set guards about Thy city all the day   and night.
So make as clear as day the grey   of night.
And it came to pass at midnight.

VA-AMARTEM ZEVACH PESACH
AND YE SHALL SAY
IT IS THE PASSOVER SACRIFICE [34]

God's heavenly power is declared on earth
below   on Passover,
And that this feast is chief of all we show on Passover,
For Abram saw the midnight skies aglow   on Passover.
    And say it is the Passover sacrifice.

One warm noontide God's vision to him spake on Passover,
He served the angels with unleavened cake   on Passover,
Then hastened to his herd for the festival's sake on Passover.
    And say it is the Passover sacrifice.

When Sodom sinned, it was destroyed by fire on Passover,
Matzot were baked by Lot, escaped from the
pyre   on Passover,
Through Egypt's length and breadth Thou didst
pass in ire   on Passover.
    And say it is the Passover sacrifice.

Then when her firstborn were at midnight
slain   on Passover,
Thou didst pass over homes where blood
showed plain   on Passover
On Israel's doors, the angel of death to restrain on Passover.
    And say it is the Passover sacrifice.

Jericho's walls were razed, though guarded well on Passover,
An omer loaf did Midian's fall foretell   on Passover,
And Put and Lud in conflagration fell   on Passover.
    And say it is the Passover sacrifice.

Hadassah called a three-day fast for prayer on Passover,
Haman hung fifty cubits in the air   on Passover,
All Israel's foes a doubledoom must bear   on Passover,
Then show Thy might, Thy holiness declare   on Passover.
    And say it is the Passover sacrifice.

(If the children have fallen asleep, wake them now for this last song—their favorite. After that tuck them into bed!)

*Part of the fun of this song is in trying to fit all the syllables in where they belong. Enjoy yourself!

V'ata chalba v'nashach l'shunra, d'achlah l'gad'ya, d'zabin abba bit'ray zuzay, Chad gad'ya, Chad gad'ya.

V'ata chutra v'hiccah l'chalba, d'nashach l'shunra, d'achlah l'gad'ya, d'zabin abba bit'ray zuzay, chad gad'ya, chad gad'ya.

V'ata nura v'saraf l'chutra, d'hiccah l'chalba, d'nashach l'shunra, d'achlah l'gad'ya, d'zabin abba bit'ray zuzay, chad gad'ya, chad gad'ya.

V'ata maya v'chavah l'nura, d'saraf l'chutra, d'hiccah l'chalba, d'nashach l'shunra, d'achlah l'gad'ya, d'zabin abba bit'ray zuzay, chad gad'ya, chad gad'ya.

V'ata tora v'shata l'maya, d'chavah l'nura, d'saraf l'chutra, d'hiccah l'chalba, d'nashach l'shunra, d'achlah l'gad'ya, d'zabin abba bit'ray zuzay, chad gad'ya, chad gad'ya.

V'ata hashochet v'shachat l'tora, d'shata l'maya, d'chavah l'nura, d'saraf l'chutra, d'hiccah l'chalba, d'nashach l'shunra, d'achlah l'gad'ya, d'zabin abba bit'ray zuzay, chad gad'ya, chad gad'ya.

V'ata mal'ach hamavet v'shachat l'shochet, d'shachat l'tora, d'shata l'maya, d'chavah l'nura, d'saraf l'chutra, d'hiccah l'chalba, d'nashach l'shunra, d'achlah l'gad'ya, d'zabin abba bit'ray zuzay, chad gad'ya, chad gad'ya.

V'ata ha-Kadosh Baruch Hu, v'shachat l'mal'ach hamavet, d'shachat l'shochet, d'shachat l'tora, d'shata l'maya, d'chavah l'nura, d'saraf l'chutra, d'hiccah l'chalba, d'nashach l'shunra, d'achlah l'gad'ya, d'zabin abba bit'ray zuzay, chad gad'ya, chad gad'ya.

(And in English we sing:)

One kid, one kid that father bought for two zuzim. One kid, one kid.

And the cat came and ate the kid that father bought for two zuzim. One kid, one kid.

And the dog came and bit the cat that ate the kid that father bought for two zuzim. One kid, one kid.

And the stick came and beat the dog that bit the cat that ate the kid that father bought for two zuzim. One kid, one kid.

And the fire came and burned the stick that beat the dog that bit the cat that ate the kid that father bought for two zuzim. One kid, one kid.

And the water came and quenched the fire that burned the stick that beat the dog that bit the cat that ate the kid that father bought for two zuzim. One kid, one kid.

And the ox came and drank the water that quenched the fire that burned the stick that beat the dog that bit the cat that ate the kid that father bought for two zuzim. One kid, one kid.

And the slaughterer came and slaughtered the ox that drank the water that quenched the fire that burned the stick that beat the dog that bit the cat that ate the kid that father bought for two zuzim. One kid, one kid.

And the Angel of Death came and slew the slaughterer that slaughtered the ox that drank the water that quenched the fire that burned the stick that beat the dog that bit the cat that ate the kid that father bought for two zuzim. One kid, one kid.

And the Holy One, blessed is He, came and killed the Angel of Death that slew the slaughterer that slaughtered the ox that drank the water that quenched the fire that burned the stick that beat the dog that bit the cat that ate the kid that father bought for two zuzim. One kid, one kid.

Let us say the prayer Y'shua taught us:
(in Hebrew and English)

Aveenu shebashama-yim,
Yitkadash sh'mecha.
Tavo malchut'cha.
Yay-asseh r'tson'cha
K'vashama-yim ken ba-aretz.
Et-lechem chukaynu ten lanu ha-yom,
Us'lach lanu et chovotaynu
Kee sol'chim gam anachnu l'cha-yavaynu.
V'al t'vee-aynu liy'day niss-yon,
Kee im hatseelaynu min hara.
Kee l'cha hammamlachah
V'hagg'vurah v'hattiferet
L'ol'may olamim.

Amen.

Our Father in heaven,
Hallowed be Your name.
Your kingdom come.
Your will be done
On earth as it is in heaven.
Give us this day our daily bread.
And forgive us our sins,
For we also forgive everyone who is
    indebted to us.
And do not lead us into temptation,
But deliver us from the evil one.
For Yours is the kingdom and the power
    and the glory forever.

Amen.

(Synthesis of Matthew 6:9-13 and Luke 11:2-4)

PART IV

PART IV

A MESSIANIC CELEBRATION

ברכ

BIBLIOGRAPHY

Blackman, Philip, *Mishnayoth* (seven volumes). London: Mishna Press (L.M. Schoenfeld), 1951-1956. Volume II *Moed*, 1952; *Pesachim* pages 161-222. Text in Hebrew and English with helpful notes.

Danby, Herbert, editor and translator. *Pesachim. In The Mishnah,* 136-151, 1933. Oxford University Press, 1933 & 1983.

Daube, David, *He That Cometh*, London Diocesan Council for Christian Jewish Understanding, St. Botolph's Church, Aldgate, London, 1966. An important contribution to our knowledge of the Last Supper and to the claims Jesus made at Capernaum (John 6).

Epstein, Isidore, (editor) *The Babylonian Talmud.* London: Soncino Press, 1938. The Soncino Press also has an office in New York. Having printed the whole Talmud in English, including the Minor Tractates which came out in 1965, the press is now producing volumes in a Hebrew-English edition. E.G. the volume containing Tractates Sukkah and Moed Katan (1984) printed in USA by Gross Brothers Printing Co., 3125 Summit Avenue, Union City, NJ 07087.

Freedman, H. (translator) *Pesachim*, 1938. Invaluable! All the other Tractates of the Talmud are available.

Rosen, Ceil and Moishe, *Christ in the Passover.* Chicago: Moody Press, 1978.

Raphael, Chaim, *A Feast of History.* New York: Simon and Schuster, 1972.

The Holy Bible, New King James Version. Containing the Old and New Testaments, Nashville: Thomas Nelson Publishers, 1979, 1980, 1982.

ADDITIONAL NOTES

In the New Testament:

1. Joseph and Mary with Jesus, age 12, made their usual pilgrimage to Jerusalem (Luke 2:41-51). Only there could the Passover sacrifice be offered (Deuteronomy 16:5-6).

2. First cleansing of the Temple by Jesus (John 2:13-25). Galileans had seen what he had done at the feast (John 4:45).

3. Feast of Unleavened Bread at Capernaum. Jesus said, "'I am the bread of life . . . the living bread which came down from heaven'" (John 6:35, 48, 51).

4. Jesus rode into Jerusalem the day that the paschal lambs were selected and assigned to each member of a group intending to observe the Passover (Matthew 21:1-11; Mark 11:1-10; Luke 19:28-44; John 12:1; 12-15).

5. Jesus cleansed the Temple. (Mark 11:11-17; Matthew 21:12-13; Luke 19:45-46. Compare removal of leaven, Exodus 12:15 and 13:7.)

6. Passover preparations and the Last Supper (Matthew 26:17-30; Mark 14:12-26; Luke 22:7-39; John 11:55; 12:1; John 13-17).

7. Jesus was betrayed and crucified (Matthew 26-27; Mark 14-15; Luke 22-23; John 18-19).

8. Peter was imprisoned before Passover. Released by an angel of the Lord while the church was praying for him, he went to the prayer meeting (and perhaps a Passover meal?) at the house of John Mark's mother (Acts 12:1-19).

9. Paul at Philippi during the Days of Unleavened Bread (Acts 20:6).

Old Testament references are too numerous to list here. Key chapters include: Exodus 1-15, Leviticus 23, Numbers 28, Deuteronomy 16, Joshua 5, II Chronicles 30 and 35, Ezra 6, Ezekiel 45, Psalms 78, 81, 105.

[1] Born ten generations after Ezra. Though wealthy, of noble birth and of keen intellect, he was a man of great humility. Appointed Nasi at age 18, he delayed taking office because of his youthful appearance. Legend declares that by a miracle his hair and beard turned white overnight. He then looked like a septuagenarian, yet humbly confessed inability to assert authoritatively that the *shema* should be said at night as well as by day. Then Ben Zoma expounded Deuteronomy 16:3 to him: "Remember the day of thy departure from Egypt *all* the days of thy life —*kol y'may cha-yecha.*"

R. Elijah ben Solomon, the Vilna Gaon (1721-1797), explains in his commentary on *Mishnah B'rachot* that the word "kol" may mean either "all" or "whole." Thus Ben Zoma read the phrase to mean "the *whole* of the days of thy life"; the Exodus should be remembered both day and night.

With the word "kol" in mind, the Sages looked beyond the normal span of life, interpreting the phrase to mean that even when Messiah had come it was our duty to remember the Exodus.

[2] The listing of the order of service rhymes to aid memory:

KADDESH	Sanctification
UR'CHATZ	Celebrant washes
KARPAS	Dip parsley
YACHATZ	Divide matzah
MAGGEED	Narrative
RACH'TZAH	All wash
MOTZEE	Bless bread
MATZAH	Bless matzah

MAROR	Bitter herb
KORECH	Sandwich (matzah & bitter herb)
SHULCHAN ORECH	Table set for meal
TSAPHOON	Hidden aphikoman uncovered
BARECH	Blessing for meal
HALLEL	Praise
NEERTZAH	Acceptance

[3] The chagigah of the 14th Nisan is eaten first so that when the paschal lamb is eaten later the appetite has already been satisfied; for if the company is large there may be for each person only a small portion of the pesach—but at least *k'za-yit*, the size of an olive—to enable each to fulfil their obligation. This chagigah, like the pesach, must come from a flock not a herd, be a yearling male, and be eaten roasted only by those who have been registered (Pesachim 70a).

[4] The three in unity, although spatially close to one another, are separated. Each in its own compartment has a special significance and proclaims a particular truth. All represent heavenly gifts. Two represent the manna that sustained life in the wilderness and the lechem mishneh —double portion—gathered each sabbath eve. The third, designated lechem onee—bread of humility or of affliction—directs hearts to the One who gives eternal life to those partaking of him, because they dwell in him and he in them. This matzah, lying between the other two, symbolized the coming Messiah until Jesus identified himself with it. Since then it has symbolized both the One-who-has-come and the One-who-is-to-come-again.

The commonly held idea that the matzot represent the three parts of Jewry (Cohen, Levi and Israel) was suggested comparatively recently (16th century) by the mystics of Safed. They may also remind us of the Trinity: Father, Son and Holy Spirit. Over the uppermost wafer we make the motzee, giving thanks to the Father who gives us our daily bread. Over the portion set aside of the middle wafer, symbolic of the bread of life that came down from heaven—redeemer and savior—we make the special matzah blessing and partake of the aphikoman as our final act of identification with the Lamb of God. We remember that outside Jerusalem in ancient days the aphikoman was eaten as a symbol of the paschal lamb. Since the destruction of the Temple and the cessation of Passover sacrifices, it has for all Jewry remained the paschal symbol.

The Holy Spirit, loving gift of God, guides and strengthens. We distribute the third matzah—the sop—as a gift of love. At the seder a father will look around for the one he loves most to whom he wishes to give the sop. Naturally he hands it to the mother of the family. Over this matzah we pronounce no blessing. How we act in response to God's spiritual gifts may determine whether we receive blessing or not.

[5] In John 6:53-58: "Then Jesus said to them, 'Most assuredly, I say to you, unless you eat the flesh of the Son of Man and drink His blood, you have no life in you. Whoever eats My flesh and drinks My blood has eternal life, and I will raise him up at the last day. For My flesh is food indeed, and My blood is drink indeed. He who eats My flesh and drinks My blood abides in Me, and I in him. As the living Father sent Me, and I live because of the Father, so he who feeds on Me will live because of Me. This is the bread which came down from heaven—not as your fathers ate the manna, and are dead. He who eats this bread will live forever.'"

A Jew should not partake of animal blood, thus partaking of its carnal life and nature (Deuteronomy 12:15-16, 23-25), but we do desire the spiritual life of Y'shua to flow through us so that we may live in him and he in us (Galatians 2:20). And so we drink from the Cup of Blessing after supper, remembering him as he commanded.

[6] Hidden from the Romans in a cave for 13 years after the defeat of Bar Cochba (135 AD), R. Shimon had much time to speculate on heavenly mysteries concerning God, Torah, the universe and humanity's place in it. According

115

to Moses de Leon (13th century) of Granada, Spain, who compiled the fundamental book of Jewish Kabbalism, the *Zohar*, R. Shimon was the original author. Yet, being written in Hebrew and Aramaic, it seems to be the product of many minds.

Ordained by his teacher, R. Akiba, R. Shimon's *Hillula* is celebrated yearly on Lag b'Omer (18th Iyar) at Meron. One of his many famous sayings refers to the three crowns: of Torah, of priesthood and of kingdom, but he says, "the crown of a good name excels them all."

[7] Only the Celebrant now washes his hands, not as a ritual, for no blessing is said, but as a courtesy before handling the food about to be distributed. There is also some possibility that wine from Kiddush may have spilt onto the Celebrant's hands. The wine should not come in contact with the lechem onee which is soon to be divided.

Some Pharisees complained that Jesus ate with *ritually* uncleansed hands. We cannot imagine that they were in fact unwashed. He was drawing attention to the truth that ritual is not enough and that cleanliness of mind and intention is as important.

[8] The Aramaic wording suggests that it was composed during the Babylonian captivity, when for Judeans to return to the homeland was impossible. "This year we celebrate here: next year, we hope, in the Land of our Ancestors. Now we are bondfolk: Next year may we be a free people."

The physically free may be in spiritual bondage. We may interpret this ancient declaration as an admission that we have still to become the best that each can be under the guidance of Torah and of the Holy Spirit. Here we have no lasting city, but we seek the city that is to come (Hebrews 13:14). There remains yet a sabbath rest for the people of God. Until we are utterly faithful and obedient, we still have to labor to enter that rest (Hebrews 4:9-11).

Let all who are hungry come and eat. Messianic blessing, like daily bread, must be shared. As the lechem onee is divided in preparation both for the beginning of the meal and, as aphikoman, for its completion, we think of others in need. The care of the poor and needy is a basic necessity. "Let *all* who are hungry . . ." Judaism prescribes the obligation of feeding the animals of our household before we ourselves sit down to a meal. At Pesach especially, as for every sabbath, the poor must be supplied with everything necessary for the full enjoyment of the festival.

[9] Another version of this passage is quoted in Montefiore and Loewe's *Rabbinic Anthology* (Macmillan, 1938, page 96): "God said to Moses, 'Dost thou not notice that I dwell in distress when the Israelites dwell in distress? Know from the place whence I speak with thee, from the midst of thorns, it is as if I stand in their distresses.'" The rabbis frequently quote Isaiah 63:9, "In all their affliction He was afflicted," and Psalm 91:15, "I will be with him in trouble." This latter verse is quoted by Rashi on Exodus 3:2 to indicate what was in consonance with God's speaking from the thornbush.

[10] Montefiore and Loewe (page 13) further quote from the same Midrash: "R. Joshua ben Karha said, 'God spoke from a thornbush to teach that there is no place where the *shechinah* is not, not even a thornbush.'"

We ourselves affirm that the shechinah was not absent from the head crowned with thorns.

[11] Each inanimate symbol has its recognized, appreciated place. When the second cup is raised in thanksgiving, to emphasize the redemptive power of God, the matzot are covered. Like the individual instruments of an orchestra, all the symbols have their moments of emphasis. God used all of them in concert to achieve his ends; therefore, give God alone the glory. Even the humblest person has his hour of significance, nor is there anything that has not its place, its purpose and importance in God's plan (Aboth 4:3).

[12] Romans 6:22; Jeremiah 31:13; John 8:12; I Peter 2:9; Colossians 1:13.

[13] Yet rejoicing may be mixed with sadness for a foe fallen without being reconciled. Consequently, on the latter days of Passover, Hallel is somewhat shortened; Psalms 115:1-11 and 116:1-11 are omitted, thus regretfully recalling the host of Egypt drowned in the Sea of Reeds. Correspondingly, we do not drink a full Cup of Thanksgiving, having removed token drops of wine in remembrance of the Ten Plagues. The Talmud records the legend of God, while his handiwork drowned, rebuking ministering angels who wished to utter their song of praise, "Holy, holy, holy. . ." (Isaiah 6:3). Attention is also drawn to II Chronicles 20:21, "Praise the Lord for His mercy endures forever," from which the psalmist's phrase "for He is good" has been omitted, because "the Holy One, blessed is He, does not rejoice in the downfall of the wicked"; although God *causes others to rejoice* (*yasis* in the Hiphil of Deuteronomy 28:63) when he has to punish those who willfully disobey his Torah (Sanhedrin 39b).

[14] The whole nation is intended to be God's sanctuary, every individual a temple of the Lord (Ephesians 2:19-22; I Corinthians 3:16-17, 6:19; II Corinthians 6:16).

[15] The ruins of what is described as the Inn of the Good Samaritan stand beside the road from Jericho to Jerusalem. An inn on that spot must have been known to Jesus. Until the road was straightened out comparatively recently, it was a tricky one for travelers. Bandits and thieves might have confronted one at many a bend of the route that zigzagged through the hills.

As one passes these ruins, it is sad to think that the impact of Jesus' parable concerning neighborliness and compassion had not fully reached the disciples' hearts. Off and on they had been quarrelling about personal one-upmanship from Capernaum to Jerusalem and even on their last night together at supper. Jesus must have grieved for his little flock! To recall this makes the Jericho-Jerusalem road indeed somber. Yet Jesus himself, knowing their weaknesses, never lost faith in the disciples. He knew what the Father could do with those who seemed utterly defeated; that disaster could be a prelude to spiritual renewal.

[16] Despite those unseized moments before *yetzer hatov*, the good inclination, wins over *yetzer hara*, the inclination to do ill, there is usually opportunity when sin has been committed for both repentance and restitution. Judas' tragedy was twofold: betrayal and its consequences; then, self-destruction, making it impossible, although after anguished repentance, to serve Jesus. With the Father's help Judas might have witnessed for Jesus with nobility and effect. When sin is overcome, we must as soon as possible take time for repentance, reconciliation and renewal of life and witness.

[17] "Blessed be God our Father. . . ." This prayer comes from Didache, an early Christian manual on morals and practice. It is thought by some scholars to be of Hebrew Christian origin.

[18] "Zeh guphee hannittan b'adchem." At Capernaum, Jesus spoke of "my flesh," *b'saree*, or in Aramaic *bisree* (John 6:55). Then he was emphasizing a particular aspect of his role as Messiah. He may have used this word at the Last Supper, but it seems more probable that he declared, "This is my guphee," my body, which is the word the Talmud uses describing how the paschal lamb is brought before the one who presides at the seder: "They brought before him *his body of the Passover offering*," *gupho shel pesach*, the whole carcass of the paschal lamb designated for before whomever it is placed (Mishnah Pesachim 10:3). The expression: "This is my body which is for you [who have been designated]" follows naturally, especially from one already declared to be the "lamb of God." Each person ate a piece of the lamb with a piece of matzah. To this day, the aphikoman symbolizes the paschal lamb and is, as it were, his body given to each one designated to be a partaker thereof.

At Capernaum, Jesus in his discourse seems to have had in mind the flesh of the lamb to be designated "his" which he would distribute at the seder in Jerusalem. More daringly, he indicated the self-giving nature of this action by adding to the words "he who eats my flesh," the further phrase "and drinks my blood," thus emphasizing to those claiming to be his followers the need to identify themselves completely with him, just as he was giving himself completely to them. As expected, many of his disciples responded, "This is a hard saying; who can understand it?" Then, after referring to his ascension, which must have seemed to them even more impossible, Jesus trenchantly says, "'It is the Spirit who gives life; the flesh profits nothing. The words that I speak to you are spirit, and they are life.'" Many at this point drew back, but the twelve continued with him, Peter declaring, "'You have the words of eternal life. Also we have come to believe and to know that you are the Christ, the Son of the Living God'" (John 6:60-69).

[19] His blood was shed for all, although not everyone has personally accepted this truth. Consequently, some have benefited, although salvation has been made available for *all*.

[20] "Proclaim." The Greek *kataggelete* is equivalent to the Hebrew *higgadta*, related to "haggadah"—narration, declaration, story.

[21] Revised Standard Version translates Exodus 12:42, "It was a night of watching by the Lord." Therefore we must daily keep watchful guard over God's precious Word. Observance must be an act of guardianship.

[22] "On the first day of the week"; or, some time between nightfall Saturday and dawn Sunday. If Sunday evening after dark is meant, it would correctly be termed (Jewishly speaking) the second day of the week.

[23] "Fear of the Judaean authorities." In a great many places, particularly in John, the word "Jews" is better rendered "Judaeans." We tend to forget that Judaea, Samaria and Galilee were virtually separate states. In a sense, Jewish Galileans who came to Jerusalem were foreigners. John frequently uses "Judaean" politically.

[24] "Shalom alaychem." Did Jesus use this well-beloved greeting? The disciples were so astonished that he had to repeat it.

[25] The open door reenacts history, reminiscent of Israel's readiness to leave Egypt immediately after the paschal meal and to trust God's guidance and protection in the wilderness.

[26] Hosheeana = Hosanna: "Save us, we pray Thee!" It is a cry for help, not an expression of praise, nor an equivalent to Hallelujah. Our Hosannas are "sweet," as the hymn writer declares, because they acknowledge our need for salvation and our total dependence on God as Savior.

[27] Thus the Levites greeted pilgrims to the Temple, and the pilgrims replied . . . .

[28] This reading is the author's translation/paraphrase of part of the *Nishmat*.

[29] In this medieval poem God is praised with every letter of the alphabet, with 22 in the original Hebrew; in this English version with 26.

Verse 1: **A**ddir, **B**lest

Verse 2: **C**hassid, **D**eliverer, **E**ternal, **F**aithful, **G**racious

Verse 3: **H**adur, **I**nfinite, **J**ust, **K**ing, **L**ord, **M**erciful

Verse 4: **N**a'or, **O**rdainer, **P**hysician, **Q**uickener, **R**edeemer

Verse 5: **S**agiv, **T**rue, **U**nchangeable, **V**ictor, **W**orshipful, E**X**alted, **Y**ea, **Z**enith.

In verse 5, line 3 is sung like line 2, and not like line 3 of the previous verses.

[30] This is the author's version of Kee Lo Na-Eh, Kee Lo Ya-Eh:

> 1. Praise ye the Lord,
> Who dwelleth on high;
> The companies of heaven
> Together all cry:

(CHORUS may be sung in either English or Hebrew:)

To You, yea to You;	*L'cha ul'cha*
To You for to You,	*L'cha kee l'cha*
To You e'en to You;	*L'cha af l'cha*
To You, the crowned King,	*L'cha Adonai*
Sing praises anew;	*Hamam'lachah*
To Him 'tis right,	*Kee lo na-eh*
To Him 'tis due.	*Kee lo ya-eh*

2. Great in power
   And mighty in deed,
   To serve God enthroned
   His messengers speed.

3. Righteous, but merciful,
   Gentle though just,
   He alone God
   To love and to trust.

4. Supreme is our King;
   How glorious His name!
   On earth as in heaven
   God's might we proclaim.

5. One is our God;
   A unity He—
   Father, Son, Spirit—
   Triune Deity.

[31] This is the author's version of "Echad Mee Yoday-A?"

Who knows One?
I know One. In heaven and earth our God is One.
   Chorus: One is our God in heaven and earth.

Who knows two?
I know two. God's Word is one, His covenants two.

Who knows three?
I know three. God is One, yet a Trinity.

Who knows four?
I know four. One Gospel truth in Gospels four.

Who knows five?

I know five. One Torah written, the Books of Moses (five).

Who knows six?

I know six. One day for rest, but work on six. (Ex. 20:9-11)

Who knows seven?

I know seven. One angel had incense, trumpets for seven. (Rev. 8:2-3)

Who knows eight?

I know eight. One ark wherein the Lord saved eight. (Gen. 7:13)

Who knows nine?

I know nine. One leper gave thanks; ungrateful nine. (Luke 17:12-17)

Who knows ten?

I know ten. With one "Keep-Remember," God's Words were ten. (Ex. 20:8; Deut. 5:12)

Who knows eleven?

I know eleven. One a betrayer, faithful eleven.

Who knows twelve?

I know twelve. One again added; with Matthias twelve. (Acts 1:26)

Who knows thirteen?

I know thirteen. The one God's attributes of love are thirteen. (Ex. 34:6-7)

These are the thirteen attributes referred to in the last verse of our version of "Echad Mee Yoday-a":

1. The Lord
2. The Lord
3. God
4. Merciful
5. Gracious
6. Long-suffering
7. Abounds in goodness
8. Abounds in truth
9. Keeps mercy for thousands
10. Forgives iniquity
11. Forgives transgression
12. Forgives sin
13. Acquits the penitent

Repetition of "The Lord" indicates that God remains the same merciful and forgiving God after a person has sinned as before the sin. By *iniquity*,[10] premeditated sin is meant. *Transgression*[11] is sin as rebellion or presumption. *Sin*[12] means provocation added to rebellion.

[32] Written for the centennial of The Hebrew Christian Alliance of Great Britain, May 1966. Lyrics by Eric-Peter Lipson.

[33] This piyyut on the Midrash Rabbah Exodus is an acrostic on the 22 letters of the Hebrew alphabet. It alludes to biblical events that occurred at night, some at Passover. Yannai, one of the earliest *payyetanim* known by name, who wrote it in the first half of the seventh century, probably lived in the Holy Land. This particular version was written by Eric-Peter Lipson.

References to the events mentioned in this piyyut are listed below:
Abraham's victory: Genesis 14:15
Gerar's king, Abimelech: Genesis 20:3
Laban: Genesis 31:24
Jacob: Genesis 32:29
Egypt: Exodus 11:4-6
Sisera: Judges 4:16
Sennacherib: II Kings 19:35
Bel: Isaiah 46:1
Daniel: Daniel 2:19
Belshazzar: Daniel 5:30
Daniel: Daniel 6:23
Haman: Esther 3:10, 13
King Ahasuerus: Esther 6:1
Winepresser: Isaiah 63:3
Watchman: Isaiah 21:12
Neither day nor night: Zechariah 14:7
Guards: Isaiah 62:6

[34] Like the previous poem, this piyyut also is an acrostic. Eleazar Kalir, said to be Yannai's pupil and rival, here gathers references to events which supposedly occurred during the Passover season, but in some cases happened centuries before the Exodus. Because, for instance, both

Abraham and Lot prepared unleavened cakes, "emergency" fare for the angelic messengers, the author assumes with poetic license that their visit was at Passover time! In stanza 5, Put and Lud were Egyptian provinces. This particular version was written by Eric-Peter Lipson.

[35] This ancient nursery tale was written in Aramaic, the common tongue Jesus spoke, so it is possible that he knew it as a child. It emphasizes the prophecy of Isaiah 25:8:

> He will swallow up death forever,
> And the Lord God will wipe away tears
>   from all faces;
> The rebuke of His people
> He will take away from all the earth;
> For the Lord has spoken.

It is confirmed in Revelation 21:4:

> . . . there shall be no more death . . . .

The kid represents God's people whose Father in heaven revealed to them the Ten Words and who paid a price for their full redemption. We may think of Sinai and Calvary as the two coins, zuzim. Forces of evil again and again have sought to destroy Israel; each has passed away. In God's providence, the kid was restored to life and to the service of the Lord when the world thought her rejected. Did the Almighty not often declare: "I will remember my covenant with thee . . . I will never forsake thee"?

So whatever happens, the kid continues to praise the Lord, for death is destroyed and God still exercises saving power. This is what the haggadah is all about—God's saving power and God's kingdom come.

ENDNOTES

A. *Rejoice in the Lord Always,* Evelyn Tarner
© Copyright 1967 by Sacred Songs (A Division of WORD, INC.) All Rights Reserved. International Copyright Secured. Used by Permission.

B. *The Haggadah*, executed by Arthur Szyk and edited by Cecil Roth (Jerusalem and Tel Aviv: Massadah and Alumoth, 1962).

C. *Baruch Haggever.* Traditional.

D. *Bind Us Together,* B. Gillman. (Nashville: Star Song Music. A Division of Straightway Music). Permission Requested.

E. *Behold I Stand.* Original melody by Stuart Dauermann (San Francisco: Jews for Jesus, 1985).

F. *Spirit of the Living God*, Daniel Iverson. Copyright 1935, 1963. Moody Press. Moody Bible Institute of Chicago. Used by permission.

G. *Eternally Grateful* Janie-Sue Wertheim, (San Francisco: Jews for Jesus, 1980).

H. *Come and Praise the Lord* Stuart Dauermann. (Kansas City: Lillenas Publishing Co., 1980) Permission Requested.

I. *Addir Hu.* Traditional.

J. *Havah Negeelah.* Traditional. Lyrics by Eric-Peter Lipson.

K. *Penlan.* Traditional. Lyrics by Eric-Peter Lipson.

For more information on Jewish holidays and their meanings write to:

Jews for Jesus
60 Haight Street
San Francisco, CA 94102-5895.